MOUNTAINS FOR PEACE

A MEMOIR BY

Anthony Massey

Mountains for Peace © 2024 by Anthony Massey

Mountainman Publishing LLC

Events and conversations in this book come from the author's recollections. As such, they are not intended to read as word-for-word transcripts and unequivocal facts but retold in a way designed to evoke emotion and meaning. In all cases, the author has attempted to honor the essence of dialogue and happenings as accurately as possible. Some names and identifying details have been changed to protect individuals' privacy.

979-8-9912271-0-0 (ebook)
979-8-9912271-1-7 (pbk)
Library of Congress Control Number 1-14494035071

Edited by L.A. Mitchell
Interior Design by Tabetha Hedrick
Cover Design by Hannah Zachry, Say When Studio

For information regarding speaking engagements or to book an event, email mountainmanpublishing@gmail.com

This story is dedicated to the children who have endured war and family trauma and those who have seen our human species destroy so much of the world around us. Remain hopeful. Some awaken from their sleep to try and repair the damage.

Contents

Mount Wilson 14,246' | El Diente 14,159'

Prologue

The Organ Pipes, a vertical cluster of towering igneous rock, rise on the brittle traverse that connects Mount Wilson and El Diente in Colorado's San Juan Mountain range. Nature's architectural magnificence. Like their instrumental counterpart, the Pipe's notes inspire euphoria, accompany pain, and summon prayer.

All present at death.

I know because I was there, pleading with death to let me live one more day.

Long before I set a goal to summit all of Colorado's Fourteeners, peaks that brag an elevation beyond fourteen-thousand feet, Africa collided with North America, seas sloshed through and drained, and volcanic explosions of ash and rock exposed magma that contained the rich and desirable minerals that put Colorado in the history books. Hard but fine-grained rock stretched upward at the root of these volcanoes but never quite reached the surface. Someone invited glaciers to the geological party, where ice whittled these towering rocks into sharp edges and steep, class-four walls that would as soon fracture as allow passage. Long before I set a goal to summit the elite of what these events left behind, I collided, endured fire and ice, aimed for the surface, and shaved away at the brittle bits below.

Unlike the mountains, I refused to fracture.

Few Fourteener faces in Colorado are as naked to the elements as the Mount Wilson/El Diente connection. The dramatic terrain is already a powder keg to the right atmospheric conditions, but it doesn't guarantee a spark. I would be fine; it wasn't much further. I just needed another hour of calm weather to reach the summit. The previous day, I'd driven seven hours across the entire damned state to get here.

I had pushed, determined to crest despite the late-season calendar date, the overcast sky, and the robust winds. I was confident the forecasted low-pressure system wasn't due for the next twelve hours. I had pushed solo because that's who I am.

Climbers logic always seems to make sense until it doesn't. If you have another climber along, you reason things better, but for me, it was like the ultimate salesperson, Zig Zigler, on why he liked talking to himself. Reinforcing chatter in my head told me, *You can do it. You have time to reach that second peak and get back down before all hell breaks loose.*

Less than an hour from the top, the sky shattered wide and high. Thunder split my eardrums and fisted my heart. Snowflakes rode the forty-knot gusts. Hairs on my body rose and saluted the electric ambush. I was hours above the dense aspen forests with nowhere to cower, a whip-thin human lightning rod of Irish messiness, baggage not strapped to my shoulders, and advanced disappointment.

I hugged the underside of a rocky outcropping, a razor's edge shelf with little room for error. In a blink, maybe two, the temperature plummeted. If there was one thing I knew about the powder kegs of the Rocky Mountains, it was that their blast was quick, and I could be staring down the sun in the next quarter-hour.

So I waited.

Sunlight did not circle back, but the wave that coated the rocks in fine powder and ice passed within thirty minutes. I breathed easy again, stretched from my precarious crouch, and stopped cataloging my life's poorest decisions.

I studied what I could see of the ridge through the cloud deck. El Diente, Spanish for *the tooth*, seemed an appropriate name for the vicious bite it had taken out of my quest. This was my third attempt, and it was right there.

Right. There.

Like a beautiful Greek siren, the summit sang to this hybrid Odysseus. *Yoooou can make it. Ignooooore the tempest.*

I added layers of clothing from my backpack, including a second pair of gloves. It was absurd, really, but the heady cocktail of thirty-three peaks of mountaineering experience and adrenaline desensitized the brain to the irrational. Instead of descending, I pushed things farther.

The last stretch on El Diente is a bitter enemy—narrow and loose, the rim like the final gauntlet before a slippery footfall to Hell. Frozen, the traverse is even worse.

Overhead, the sky unleashed another wave of brute force. High winds. Temperature drop. Horizontal snow. I scrambled down a bit and aimed for the nearest large outcropping. My hands shook—nerves or first-stage hypothermia, I couldn't say. A churning fog of gray and white smothered everything within sight. I had screwed myself out of every option.

I had ascended right into an exit point. One of several that most of us get in a lifetime. I cannot say for sure if the decision is ours to seize or leave behind. All I know is that life's storms come in waves, the elements will always expose us, and the end is a solo endeavor.

I pulled my cell phone from my pack. Absurd, really. The closest tower to ping a signal had to be a galaxy and a half away.

Twelve percent battery.

One bar.

Oh. I bit the glove off my right hand. My fingers slipped across the keypad. I pressed it to my ear.

"State police, what's your emergency?" came a man's voice.

Warm tears gathered.

The end is a solo endeavor.

Until it isn't—a solo *or* an end.

Mount Princeton 14,197'

Chapter One

Grand notions often have significant beginnings: professors who challenge their students to step out of their comfort zones, a life-changing diagnosis with an expiration date, births and deaths and other significant bookmarks to our journey.

Mine was not nearly so splendid.

In 1990, I moved my family to the foothills northwest of Denver. The major electronics company I worked for had launched a government division and offered me the Colorado position and a pay increase. I'd stand at the west-facing window of our new home, stare out at the white-capped backcountry, and long to be there. This has always been a thing for me. Wherever I am, I want to be elsewhere.

Even better if I'm in nature. Best yet, if I'm in spaces where few have been. Damaging myself is secondary. That's a thing, too.

Craig Huey offered me friendship shortly after my arrival. We shared a love of the outdoors—his more of the sea than the sky. He was a natural sailor with a wide stance, a slight build, an easy smile, and at only thirty-five, a prematurely grizzled silver-and-black crown of hair. His quiet embrace of discomfort and unrelenting positivity made him the best first mountaineering partner I could have asked for.

Around the time Craig and I discussed the possibility of my first Fourteener, my second daughter, Elyse, was born. There was a correlation—this escalation of risk. The threat of plunging off a mountain is nothing compared to taking on the responsibility of a life. Parenthood starts with hope, leans heavily on instinct, tries not to acknowledge fear, and is one of the greatest emotional risks in a lifetime. I needed the external pull of the mountains to balance out the inner ledge of fatherhood. The nimble but durable backpack I purchased and loaded with Craig's suggested contents proved easy. The only equipment I had packed for a parental journey was a topographic emotional map highlighting where *not* to go.

Mount Princeton, part of the Collegiate Peaks range, sits close to the state's center along the Arkansas River Valley and rises dramatically on the drive from Leadville to Buena Vista. I believed my Stairmaster and bike conditioning to be ideal training for the physical test of five thousand vertical feet in seven miles. I was forty, agile, and motivated by itches inside that I had not yet come close to scratching.

Craig had a talent for breaking anything into a process, an approach that inspired confidence where it did not yet exist. His knowledge of Colorado's mountains was extensive but not boisterous. At Colorado Mountain College in Glenwood Springs, his professor and mentor was Roger Paris (pronounced Paree), a Frenchman who was a ski instructor, former world champion kayaker, and a Chamonix-Mont-Blanc mountain guide. An influencer at that level of outdoor accomplishment elevated Craig's outdoor prowess. By the time we befriended each other, Craig had already summited twenty Fourteeners.

At the Grouse Canyon Trailhead, the July day dawned clear and warm. I charge up the trail like the ghost of William Libby (Princeton grad responsible for the mountain's first recorded ascent in 1877) possessed me. Craig followed at a diligent pace. Distance between us stretched. About two hours into our hike, a fiery burn in my right knee flared and ebbed away the upper reaches of my energy. I slowed to a more reasonable speed.

Every partner climb is different. I strive to keep chatter to a minimum. There's little space between the lungs and throat for *how's the wife and kids* or *get a load of that view* when you're hungry for air. As Mount Princeton kicked my ass, Craig closed the gap. Like a parent waiting out a teachable moment while his child stumbles into mind-numbing failure, Craig said nothing of my frantic pace.

I'm told the view at Mount Princeton's twelve-thousand-foot tree line is breathtaking. I wouldn't know. Heat radiated from my right knee and kept me hyper-focused on the immediate six feet of ground. For inner motivation, I summoned my track and cross-country years in high school—those punishing training days inside an invincible body. As a runner who earned my only varsity letter on an All-Eastern District cross-country team, I had been extraordinarily common in athletics. Three decades on, my body was neither bulletproof nor boundless. On the mountain, I reached a point where forward progress meant a high step with my left leg and dragging my right boot sole like a carcass.

We summited around noon. By this point, I was certain Craig wanted me to limp off the closest ledge. With a small pile of rocks and some unnecessary artifact from my pack, he might have eulogized: *here went Anthony, who complained his way to death.*

Instead, he high-fived me. "Congratulations, man. Your first Fourteener."

I tried to distract myself from exhaustion by viewing hundreds of miles of snow-capped peaks—my first real Rocky Mountain high. Exhales pushed my pain into the thin air.

The rest of the adventure was downhill. Down was good. Down was a breeze, right?

On the descent, my right knee locked up, a buildup of lactic acid. Forward movement was no longer an option. Many unpalatable scenarios presented themselves: an expensive and embarrassing mountain rescue, a romantic couples-carry down the trail on Craig's back, planting myself like an evergreen, without camping equipment for days until my limbs no longer betrayed me.

I sampled one final option.

First priority: keep balanced on a steep trail while looking backward.

Second priority: stop, gather my breath through gritted teeth, step.

Third—or maybe first—priority: maintain my dignity.

After hours of scuttling backward like a mountain goat with a warped internal compass, we reached the tree line. Craig found me a large stick to use as a crutch.

Much later than expected, we reached the car at the trailhead. My body felt like it had tumbled off Princeton's east face. Ever the patient man, Craig settled me into his SUV's upholstered seat with food and water and gave me time to recover before driving home.

Descending rear-first wasn't an elegant inauguration to my quest, but life is best understood looking backward.

Unfortunately, it must be lived forward.

My new position as a government accounts manager required extensive travel—more than one hundred thousand flight miles per year. I spent a third of my year in hotels. I learned military speak and dropped acronyms with a borrowed confidence until I owned them. Engaging Department of Defense clients became my specialty. Military bases became grounding stops on my path to success within the global manufacturing company. But it was a hamster wheel of illusion, an overachieving sleight of hand to distract others from my dirty little secret.

I was not degreed. Nothing more than a high school diploma and a happenstance stumbling into a career.

Supervisors knew this, of course. But my colleagues saw an educated, ambitious family man passionate about travel, meeting new clients, and…electronics. A farther distance from true North did not exist. I disliked the sterile and impersonal confines of airports and hotels. I am an introvert who feels tremendous inner turmoil to chat someone up. And electronics? Give me a paper trail map and some hours to burn, any day.

Feeling like a second-class citizen in a company climate where everyone was educated forced me to think outside the box. I couldn't chat up alma maters or other hollow points of polite conversation, so I made it a point to remember and chat up the passions of others. I thrived when I was given the freedom to go after a particular business angle and develop it. Not unlike studying a hulking chunk of limestone and shale and rooting out the best way to summit, I created a route that worked for me.

The heaviest imbalance to my inauthentic work life was my family.

One October evening, three-year-old Erin padded down to my basement office where I worked on rare evenings I wasn't on the tarmac, wheels up. She stared at me with her wide doe eyes, drew lines in the carpet with the footy part of her pajamas, and waited for me to finish my phone call. Eventually, she climbed back upstairs. A little later, she visited again, but I remained focused on work. Upstairs she went. Shortly after, another trip down, but I was in the same state.

"Daddy!" she demanded. "Come upstairs and love me!"

I was so taken by this expression of love and longing from my little girl that I immediately dropped everything, went upstairs, and spent the evening with her until bedtime.

If only I had learned from this teaching moment.

Some years later, her younger sister, Elyse, was asked by her elementary school teacher, "What does your daddy do?"

"My daddy works at the airport."

Me, gone, was all they knew. I had become a workaholic, afraid to be less than fully and intensely dedicated to my job. We had a comfortable home, enough income to afford us the choice to have a stay-at-home parent, and the veneer of busyness that somehow equates to life humming along on a happy frequency.

All while I was out of my depth about how to be an attentive father.

Mountaineering is a spectrum sport. At one end are the weekend warriors who strap on a day pack and climb over a few boulders. At the opposite end are the subjects of drone-shot Netflix documentaries where the young, charismatic free climber dies at the end.

My crusade occupied a safe middle. I am not a technical climber; I pick my way through the terrain. Not much more than steps up a mountain with the occasional accidental free climb because I've miscalculated a route. I climb in summer because extreme cold shifts me into a part of myself I don't enjoy, especially when my hands freeze up and stop working, and I find the changeover in footwear to crampons tedious. Ironic, I suppose—to drill down on a hobby where the air loses pressure, expands, and turns frigid. Maybe I should have pursued paper boat origami in bathwater. Ninety percent of my time on a trail is spent tapping into what my body gives me. The remaining ten percent of my climbs? Pushing aside the darkness that haunts these pages.

Nature gifts the rich terrain. The journey is either short and sweet, long and sweet, short and difficult, or long and difficult. It's my job to look for hidden revelations and respect what the mountain tells me. Intentionally pressing past difficult stretches increases the likelihood of a lethal descent. Over time, the mountain's voice becomes more apparent and the whispers more intimate.

Unpacking one reason I settled upon all of Colorado's fifty-five Fourteeners at mid-life is like trying to appreciate Boulder's Flatirons by looking through a straw.

Narrow in scope. Next to impossible.

If I craved a challenge, why not run across America? If I wanted adventure, why not an Amazon trek? If I chased altitude, why not skydiving or base jumping? And if mountaineering were my thing, why not Ranier or Everest?

After the ego bruise from Mount Princeton vanished, I fondly remembered the hike's physicality. I knew what to expect and the shortcomings of my conditioning. I loved that my first peak had kicked my ass because it established the parameters of what was possible. Heights did not intimidate me. And I learned that fewer people had accomplished all of Colorado's Fourteeners than had climbed Everest. That would put me in a select company, which seemed to justify expending the effort. It was on my doorstep, literally outside my window. Why not stay close to home and do something memorable?

These points have always been my surface answer. They hold logic and are safe. They were answers I fed to anyone who discovered my dream because I had zero intention of advertising such an endeavor on the front end. To do so would bring bad luck and the kind of attention that risked mischaracterizing my quest. Maybe I feared not finishing something I had started. But if anyone at the outset were to have sliced through my motivation and uncovered the marrow of why, my answer would have been simpler.

I began this quest because I am ordinary. Forgettable in every way, in all stages of life.

I am not an academic. My frame is stretched taffy-thin and not particularly strong. I have no talent for the arts. I am not gifted in people skills, oration, technology, swimming, or basket weaving. I had an impressive list of inadequacies and a desire to endure, to strengthen my mental fortitude like a muscle, and to make up for a history that broadcasted that I was nothing.

The field of psychology has studied the motivations of alpinism for over a century. In the sport's early days, some might have undertaken such a sport for the incomparable views from the tops of the world. With today's technology, the same panoramic experience can be found beyond the window of a 737 or on the screen in our pockets. Unfavorable weather often obscures the summit view, and the top-down perspective frequently distorts and flattens lower nearby peaks to less-than-impressive vistas. If it isn't the scenery, what is the draw to an extreme sport with potentially fatal consequences?

Mountaineers experience a sort of arrested exhaustion. The constant change of scenery, the string of decisions, and the escalating excitement as the goal draws near pushes climbers beyond the boredom that might set in with nature hikes at lower elevations. It is a dramatic but bloodless battle. Exploration in microcosm. Intricate problem solving with less oxygen. A mountain is impartial and does not discriminate. The advanced fatigue at the top, the idea that our bodies have been pushed beyond what is reasonable and sometimes what is safe, and the very juxtaposition between joy and catastrophe makes us feel alive.

Achievement reminds us of our pulse.

Then, at each apex, climbers surrender part of their souls.

I desire to feel extreme fatigue, to endure. My decisions—my control—over what happens on the mountain are a heady pleasure center in my brain because much of my life was not me. I override physical indicators to stop for reasons I don't always understand. Maybe fatigue is simply the mountain's way of telling me I'm not enough, and I refuse to accept one more truth.

I studied peak ratings, read books by experts who had gone before me, prepared myself for exhaustion and pain, measured conditions, assessed time windows to get up to elevation and back down, and set my sights on the easiest of the fifty-five first.

For those who long to be more than forgettable, the gravity is irresistible. Instinctively, I knew this as early as Mount Princeton.

And so I made myself a promise.

Today, my spirituality lies at the intersection of nature and things I cannot yet articulate. I attribute this to my early memories of the outdoors.

As a five-year-old boy in Northeast Hampshire, England, I developed the habit of leaving Yateley Hall Covenant School on a whim. The dark pond blanketed in lily pads at the far end of the property drew me. In my limited capacity, I considered who I was and how I fit into my spaces. I wondered how blooms could sprout from darkness and suspected that nature somehow held all the answers.

My teachers feared I would fall in and drown.

I feared that I wouldn't—that I would forever occupy a space void of the elements I believed were essential. A space not unlike the spiritually bankrupt interior behind the four-hundred-year-old Catholic school walls.

Yateley Hall stood on a formerly moated site that had been continuously occupied since the thirteenth century. The grounds also contained a *ha-ha*, also known as a sunk fence. This recessed landscape design creates a vertical barrier, particularly on one side, while preserving an uninterrupted view of the landscape from the other side. The term *ha-ha* is thought to have stemmed from Louis XIV of France's son, whose governess used such a barrier to prevent the boy from approaching the drop in elevation for fear of injury. Rumor has it that the child said, "Ha-ha, *this* is what I'm supposed to be afraid of?"

As a Dubliner, my Catholic mother carried the fresh, stale wounds of four hundred years of British occupation. She wasn't permitted to marry my father, a Protestant American, without a dispensation from the Catholic Church in Rome. In this signed agreement, my parents agreed to raise all future children as Catholic. I didn't know I was in a Protestant country, but I knew Catholic nuns taught me. Mom never passed up an opportunity to remind us boys that the Protestant faith was started by "a whoring king and a breakaway priest."

The pond allowed me time alone. I was a skinny kid with the Queen's accent, bony knees, and an intense dislike of polyester shorts. For an outdoor play of the *Pied Piper of Hamelin*, I told the nuns that if they made me wear my uniform shorts, I would go home, get my gun, and shoot them. I was the only one in the performance who wore long pants.

When it was time for our family to move to the States, the Mother Superior wrote a letter intended for my future instructors: *We are sorry to lose Anthony. He is an interesting, lovable boy who must be approached with understanding.*

She attached a report card.

Gym: quite good but is sometimes slow to join in activities.

Games: improved but still needs to be quicker on his feet.

History: quite interested in stories

Nature: listens carefully

Somehow, five-year-old Anthony understood me more than my grown self.

Chapter Two

ONE YEAR INTO THE QUEST

Sunshine and Redcloud are buddy class one and class two peaks that sit a mile and a half apart in the San Juan Range. For someone on a Fourteener quest to summit one and not traverse to the other would be foolish. The twelve-mile combo starts with a forested quarter mile that is ambitious in elevation, winds past the bright white rocks of Silver Creek's headwaters, and finishes on a bald summit that more closely resembles the face of Mars than Colorado's high country. The dramatic red dirt, caused by the oxidization of the iron in the rock, was the backdrop to the first Fourteener where I didn't feel like a liability to Craig. My enhanced conditioning had paid off, and the day was gorgeous. Checking two peaks off the list in one day was a total rush.

Back at the car, we drove the three hours to Leadville and camped to tackle Mount Sherman the next day. Sherman is widely considered the easiest of all Fourteeners. It's a stripped-down, tan-and-snow-colored bleak rise with little to see beyond the scraps of bygone mining operations, massive scree fields, and a false summit that gets dicey but barely strays into class two territory. For all that the scenery is forgettable—everything but the panoramic vista at the top—Sherman is significant in my quest for a reason that never fails to bring on a hint of wistful sadness.

On the descent, Craig taught me to tuck an ice axe backward under my armpit and glissade down a snow field. Like brakes on an alpine coaster, the more I leaned into the cut, the slower my progress. It was an extraordinary way to experience a mountain, even if the stress of losing control and rocketing into the boulder field at Sherman's base caused me to slide across the snowpack in gentle and guarded bursts.

I wish I had let go more. Such an exhilarating ride that would rarely come again.

In fifty-five peaks, Sherman was one of the only times I used an ice axe.

In the nearly thirty years since, Colorado's expansive snow fields are becoming a distant memory. As global temperatures rise and winters shorten, the snowpack is vulnerable. More high-altitude storms fall as rain, and more melting occurs between systems. In another thirty years, likely less, Colorado's resorts will open to skiers fifty percent fewer days than when I moved to the state. Despite being someone who doesn't particularly like the cold, I mourn the old climate like a snow leopard in the tropics.

The early Fourteeners met a different Anthony. I started a journal and checked off peak names and dates as if I had conquered them in battle. Me versus the mountain. I worried about the harder climbs to come, calculating time and logistics from base camp because some of them were more remote. I obsessed over the windows of time to get back down the mountain, a singularity of focus that had me squandering my time at the summit. Results over process. Soon, I realized Craig was not as driven about his Fourteeners. Though immensely grateful for his knowledge and experience, I yearned to strike out independently.

Alone was a place my father had taught me was safest.

Some mountaineers see the impossible. Hallucinations of climbers with brightly colored parkas and desperate tears of ice in their beards who appear for a stretch and give advice like *jump off the south face—it's a faster descent* before the blinding snow consumes them. Few things about this mountain psychosis are related to the usual trappings of high-altitude sickness: headaches, nausea, and brain swelling. These phantom mountain guides exist above twenty-three thousand feet to recalibrate good sense and usher death.

My mountain ghosts didn't lead me so high.

Though my father never set foot on a mountain, he was my first phantom guide. He existed to recalibrate good sense and usher in those of us who occupied his trench, all manner of pain—spiritual, emotional, and bodily. Often, when I scaled peaks dressed in a brightly colored parka and worn boots, with no space left between the lungs and throat, absurdity crept in, and I'd wish for a brush of blinding snow to consume him.

Climbers like to believe that when our boots hit the terrain, we develop the superpower to push the junk aside, that fresh oxygen cleanses, and that nature heals.

But we are liars.

Warren Massey dropped out of high school in the tenth grade to join the Navy. After his twenty-one-year stint in the military, he retired as a Chief Petty Officer, where he had earned his GED. He was discharged and became an aviation mechanic for a major Dayton, Ohio, company that serviced Chinook helicopters. The company sent him to Vietnam as a civilian to provide mechanical support for their fleet during the war.

He didn't last long.

Details of a sketchy physical altercation that resulted in a traumatic neck injury had the company sending him home within five months. He then parked himself at a desk job at the Army Corp of Engineers, where he received the first stable income of his life. He finished this career arranging paper clips and receiving disciplinary action for his behavior with colleagues. Combative and adversarial, his biggest hurdle in life was interpersonal relations. After his time in the Corps, his world grew small. He sold used cars, worked at Sears, and tried his hand at investment trading.

His rootlessness became our family burden. Different countries, different schools, different realities, depending on how insecure he felt when facing life's adversity. By the time I was eleven, we had moved six times. The path of least resistance became caution and introspection.

Having settled in Virginia Beach, Virginia, my father became a frequent flyer at the city's General Hospital: an automobile accident involving a Valium-and-alcohol cocktail and a brick wall, a diagnosis of *general brain disease* after the self-reporting of massive head trauma as a young man, depression and chronic insomnia, and the massively understated *conflict* with his wife.

Out of his four sons, I most resemble him—our whip-thin build, our facial structure, wide-set eyes, small mouth, everything but his dark hair. Because he often stared back at me in the mirror, I stepped through life with a deliberateness to become a man and a father that was not him.

Some of my earliest memories in England involved climbing into the backseat of his car at dawn and curling up on the seat. My father would turn over the engine and putter down the gravel road on his way to work. For a bit, the radio lifted a quiet tune or a calm voice reading the morning's headlines while the sun turned up its light. Eventually, he would discover his stowaway, and the car would turn around without words. Birch and sycamore trees zoomed past the windows until the car rested again, and he would walk me back into the house.

I can't say why I stole away to be with him. That was before much of the pain. He had potential without any shadows, and I was outside, looking in.

So, too, was he.

Chapter Three

Two and three years into the quest

Northwest of Buena Vista, Mount Missouri sits like a saddle ridge with a tremendous view of the Sawatch Range. I'd heard it called Mount *Misery*, but I couldn't find anything on the four-hour ascent that warranted such a nickname. Old cabin remnants coming out of the forest, a bubbly creek crossing, and some fun cave-like, class 2 formations on the ridge provided the right level of difficulty for this stage of my journey.

I was on such a high that July Fourth weekend and had enough peaks behind me that I wanted to share a Fourteener with my wife,

Darlene. Far more cultured than me, I knew she would probably rather spend her time at a Broadway musical than be whipped by alpine winds and pushed to physical exhaustion. But we had always made a point to discover and respect what is loved inside those we love. For all the encouragement she had given to my quest, having her along for one piece of it seemed appropriate.

A week after Missouri, we set out for Quandary Peak near Breckenridge. According to legend, the peak was named by a group of miners in the 1860s who discovered a unique mineral on its slopes and tried, in vain, to identify the specimen. Quandary is a six-mile trek in three parts: trees, open basin trails, and a long final push at a tremendous angle to the summit. For mid-July, the mountain was surprisingly cool but clear. Beginning at almost eleven thousand feet meant we wouldn't have to gain much elevation to reach the summit, and trail information made it seem easy.

On several occasions, Darlene stopped me. "I can't keep your pace. I need to catch my breath."

Understandably, the advanced altitude proved challenging to her. Frequent delays weren't something I was used to but stopping caused me to connect with her joy of seeing the landscape change with the rising elevation. She noticed the finer details of our surroundings that I wouldn't have seen—the ink spot-like Blue Lakes, the mountain goats, salmon-colored paintbrush flowers, and snow fields. Alone, I would have kept my gaze focused on my feet and moving. This mindset was becoming a Fourteener pattern for me—singular of focus, fixed on attaining a goal, and not paying much attention to what came before. I was grateful to her for the reminder that the journey also held merit.

Crawling back into the car at the trailhead, I said, "So what did you think?"

"Go have fun, dear."

I couldn't help but laugh. So often in our relationship, I had asked her to step outside her comfort zone—black diamond skiing, whitewater rapids, extended camping jaunts. She was a great sport about Quandary. At the very least, I could sit through a production of actors in furry manes and tails pretending to be cats the next time it came around.

Quandary gave Darlene first-hand experience with the easier part of the Fourteener list. Not once did she take for granted what the peaks at the opposite end of the spectrum presented. We settled into a comfortable rhythm: she never asked me not to do something because it was dangerous, and I never left without telling her a peak name. In her words: *I have to know where to send someone to look for you if you don't come back.* Her friends often asked her how she endured the worrying. She'd simply answer, "It wouldn't be him without it."

Her *I-won't-fight-this—Go-on* attitude was a supreme and selfless gift of freedom, especially with daughters at home for us to finish raising. Near death, injury, and adversity went hand-in-hand with the quest. Beyond the few times she voiced her feminine intuition about a particular day or peak not feeling right, she never asked me to step away from my dream.

For that, for the finer details of a love well-lived, I am immensely grateful.

Climbing is a chess match. A mountain is an adversary, unyielding and flawless in all its imperfections. Peaks are dynamic and ever-changing environments that can sometimes seem to make calculated moves of opposition. Hours pass, making a delayed win that much sweeter.

One wrong decision about weather, when to push forward and when to turn back, can be the difference between a satisfying checkmate of the summit or surrendering to the elements with a disastrous outcome. As I checked peaks off my list, I learned how to read the mountain.

Now what?

Can I keep ascending?

Is that where I want to end up?

If I reach an endpoint on that ascent, is there an alternate direction?

How stable is the rock?

Such a foe has tells: the way sunlight hits a crevasse to reveal depth, slope grade, scree fields, conditions beneath a boot's sole, the visual route under constant scrutiny as the landscape tightens. A climber who fails to plan and strategize is likely a dead climber, so I researched peaks in a way that was only possible pre-internet—trail-head maps, the advice of those who had ascended before, and Gerry Roach's *Colorado Fourteeners* paperback guide, largely considered the bible for anyone undertaking the best the high country had to offer. I wasn't technical climbing, with all the extensive preparation required of such an advanced endeavor, so essentially, I engaged in a back-and-forth with the terrain. In the same way that I thrived in my career when given a goal and the freedom to get there my way, I blew past peak after peak.

Mount Belford, with my dentist, Mark, of the same surname, where I learned that I could gain one thousand feet of elevation per hour if I didn't stop except to regain my breath and sip water.

Mount Oxford, where I traversed the saddle ridge between where, sadly, a father and daughter had fallen to their deaths the prior summer, before circling back and rejoining the same dentist, who had used our two hours apart for his epiphany: mountaineering, for him, didn't tap the same reservoir of endorphins as marathon running.

Was I *that* intense?

First, Darlene bailed on the sport, then my dentist. Mark Belford wasn't the type to get retribution in the dental chair, but he reinforced my instinct to return to being a solo climber.

Mount Bierstadt's marshy willows and medium, class-2 boulders.

The iconic Mount Evans, which supports the highest paved road in North America and has since been renamed Mount Blue Sky because its former namesake governor had played a pivotal role in the Sand Creek Massacre of the Cheyenne and Arapahoe tribes. I found Evans to be amusement-park crowded due to its road access, so I quickly rooted out a descent across an open expanse of grass and rock on its large western-facing hump. In this bowl, I discovered a fully intact ram's horn, often depicted on a totem to symbolize perseverant, philosophical, and sensitive people. I took it as a personal gift from the mountain. When I returned home, I soaked it in bleach and placed it on my office shelf. It would later be joined by a Pegasus horse figurine made from steel coiled wire by a street artist in Paris. Not that I wanted to fly or leap off a mountain, but together, they somehow seemed to sum me up.

Peak after peak, I navigated the Fourteeners far better than the chess matches in other areas of my life. I picked my way through the terrain and tried not to dead end. On the mountain, the next one to three moves were limited only by my physicality and delivered a reinforcing confidence that I lacked in trials requiring a greater emotional component. Relationships and careers tend to go sideways for me.

The Fourteeners?

Right on track.

Ten summits into my quest, I took on my biggest challenge yet: Long's Peak.

For much of the year, this Fourteener remains in winter conditions. I chose a September climb when frozen precipitation is least likely, but Long's is notorious for the possibility of year-round snow and ice. The first six miles of the grueling sixteen-mile adventure is a proper hike. After, the trail opens onto Boulder Field and slows a climber's unrelenting pace to that of a scrabbler. So named for the fat cone of car and SUV-sized boulders, Boulder Field marks the entrance to the significant danger of the climb: towering, sentinel-like ridges that vault upward and split apart at a rounded opening that resembles a keyhole. Though the Keyhole Route is the only way to summit Long's without a technical climb, falling rocks, ledges, narrows, and troughs where a ropeless fall would be fatal remain an ever-present threat.

Bounding from one boulder to the next, I was an exhilarated child. Tension melted from my neck and shoulders. I spotted a stone beehive-shaped hut that marked the Keyhole's official entrance and inspected it.

The small, circular shelter had no door. Ice lingered on the stone floor. At a place where the air should feel paper thin, the space inside felt like an anchor, eerie and ghostly. I moved ahead.

I climbed through the Keyhole, ascending and descending a series of ledges and a v-cut of rock known as The Trough, a steep couloir reaching the mountain's base. I paused to breathe in the spectacular view of the Glacier Gorge, which drains its ice and snow into the numerous lakes and waterfalls of Rocky Mountain National Park.

This. This was living.

A small path cut into the side of the vertical rock on Long's south face, known as The Narrows, looked intimidating but became an easy scramble. The Homestretch is the final portion of the climb, where maneuvering over smooth, angular stabs of granite, no doubt a slick nightmare in wet conditions, is the only way to finish. Using careful hand and foot placements for a few hundred more feet, I summited and let out a gasp of relief.

Eight miles of terrain in a constant state of dramatic and consequential change.

As far as I could tell, the descent meant repeating it all in reverse. I wasn't looking forward to it. Going down was always the hardest part for me. Statistically, that sentiment tracked.

Descents are when most mountaineers make lethal decisions. The body is spent. Focus wanes on critical things like balance, foot placement, and confirming a step is stable before shifting weight. Sometimes, the descent isn't the same route as the ascent, so new problems are met with a tired mind. Fatigue leads to relaxed core muscles when they should remain tight. The day stretches long. Dehydration becomes a real possibility. Afternoon environmental conditions are often the diciest.

I took extra minutes to recharge my legs and look out over Boulder and Denver. The view of open plains to the east and the rugged interior to the west was majestic. I understood why the Fourteener was so popular. And why it was the deadliest.

I wondered if there might be an easier and quicker way down, but I couldn't see one. Looking east, at what could be a shortcut across the top of the mountain and avoiding the long route back, I saw thirteen thousand nine-hundred-foot Mount Meeker. Lacking the confidence to navigate the unfamiliar route back with what energy I had left, I retraced my route. In my car back at the trailhead, to use Irish slang, I was completely knackered from the sixteen-mile trek and nine hours of hiking.

Sadly, at that time, Long's was still just another mountain. Number eleven. A name and elevation on a list. A goal to achieve and a means to challenge myself.

Back home, I read an article by local author and historian Kenneth Jessen about the tragic history of the Keyhole Route's stone hut.

According to Jessen, in January 1925, a Denver socialite named Agnes Vaille aimed to make her name known in the predominantly male world of mountaineering. After two previous failed attempts the previous October with her climbing partner, a Swiss mountaineer named Walter Keiner, they hiked up the glacier to the ledge known as Broadway. On the direct route up the east face known as Notch Couloir, Walter cut steps into the ice for twelve straight hours. Exhaustion set in for them both, but they believed a retreat far more dangerous. They pushed ahead and summited at four in the morning, intending to descend a far easier route. But a blizzard set in—waist-deep snow, high winds, and temperatures of minus fourteen degrees. Agnes fell onto Boulder Field, unable to move. Walter fetched help. By the time they returned, Agnes had frozen to death. A member of the rescue party became disoriented in the storm and perished. Walter lived the rest of his days without most of his toes and fingers, a consequence of severe frostbite. The National Park Service constructed the shelter at the 13,400' mark above Boulder Field to memorialize Agnes, the first woman to make a winter ascent of Long's Peak's east face.

Somehow, after Agnes, Long's was no longer number eleven. A name and elevation on a list. It was a story with passion and consequence. Triumph and tragedy. Somehow, after the father and daughter, after Agnes, the mountains commanded my respect.

And I began to comply.

Darlene marked a pivotal shift in my life's trajectory. I might have remained enamored with the mountains, enmeshed in living out the day-to-day as a professional outdoorsman. I was already established in white water rafting in Virginia, West Virginia, and Maryland. I was adept at handling four and six-man ranger rafts, and I enjoyed being able to spot a rapid and anticipate the optimum angle to maneuver to achieve the desired effect. Had I been delusional about my capacity to bond with others in an outdoor setting, I would have undoubtedly become a wilderness guide. But I am a loner. I don't want the responsibility of another's life. Without a connection beyond a paycheck, I am impatient to rid myself of strangers and return to the peace and solitude where I feel most comfortable.

So it was an extraordinary happenstance that a woman had the capacity to upend me.

I found Darlene as engaging as she was beautiful. Anyone who can turn me into a good conversationalist is gifted. Beyond her intelligence and our common ground, I was attracted to her spirit of adventure and openness to experience new things. After a two-day run down the Gauley River in West Virginia, she smiled and confessed that she thought she would die on the trip.

When she found me, I was broken. In a blind span of immaturity, I had once taken society's expected road and married young. A false summit, to be sure. I carried with me the example of my parents, an annotated guidebook to a failed relationship. Five years in, we realized we were not right for each other. Ten years on, we walked away with no children. I wore the blame for the failed relationship like a down parka in the summer heat and vowed, moving forward, to be more open and to communicate in a way I did not see modeled as a child.

Darlene had the healthy foundation that I lacked. Her parents, brother, and cousins were a gift, a stasis, an example of how familial love is meant to function. We hummed along in our thirties, making a nice income and enjoying being together. Life was comfortable. Marriage was kind.

To be blessed with children was a role I didn't seek but something I am immensely grateful for.

Along with Darlene, my daughters, Erin and Elyse, amended my definition of fatherhood. I strived to shift away from the contentious side of conflict, a self-preservation holdover from the years with my father, but I was far from perfect. My communication style wasn't well-developed, more in-your-face, and there were still emotions and states of being that I didn't know what to do with—namely frustration that I was pushing myself so hard on so many fronts but still felt inadequate to the world.

Inner dissonance created pressure that only the mountains remedied.

The Fourteener quest manifested for me inside the dry world of office equipment.

In late spring of 1995, the electronics company that had promoted and moved me hired a new supervisor. Barely three months on board, a higher-up sat me down and said, "Anthony, I'm not satisfied with your performance as a manager. I don't think you're cut out for this position, and I recommend you step down."

My mouth went ten-hour Mojave-hike dry, complete with all the accompanying symptoms of a scorching level of trauma: light-headedness, headache, nausea. I had wiped the floor of my responsibilities with everything inside. I had ignored my family and acquired more flyer miles than an astronaut. Half of Colorado's best trails contained still-smoldering shrapnel of stress dished out by a company that made little more than glorified copy machines.

The richness of self-importance nearly elicited a laugh.

"On what basis?" And with not a little shedding of my self-respect, I added, "I'm willing to address any shortcomings and improve myself."

He offered little specifics. Still, I pressed for ways I could improve but was met with silence. Though he had not fired me, I was still forced to don an archery-sized target on my back. What had once been a supportive and collegial middle-management environment before his arrival turned into an adversarial, toxic, survival-of-the-fittest work climate.

For nearly a year, I projected a calmness and self-assurance to my team, those who depended on me to lead them, that I did not feel. How would I support my young family if I lost my job? I surrendered completely to my employer. No Fourteeners. Nothing but work. Ultimately, I received word I would be removed as district manager. A last-ditch appeal to the senior management that had rewarded me so richly for a job well done the six years prior resulted in an even more unsatisfactory solution: my adversary and I were to work more closely together so that I might improve my role as manager.

I had saved my job, but at what price?

Our colleague dynamic was set. Inside, I was emotional taffy. When my brother offered me an out—a way to work for him—I resigned. On my way out, to the upper managers who had supported me, I confessed in grandiose fashion that I finally felt free.

In retrospect, not my finest moment.

Even the greenest hiker alive knows that still-smoldering shrapnel starts a forest fire.

Chapter Four

FOUR YEARS INTO THE QUEST

At the summit of Snowmass Mountain, Vince pulled out his disposable plastic camera and snapped a photograph of me to mark the occasion. A cloud bank had arrived at the same time but parted briefly for the shot. With a misty-white view of the drainage basin fourteen stories below, I smiled at our fresh achievement.

The moment in time he captured on film looks like a dream.

In so many ways, it was.

Vince Bousellaire represented the full spectrum of mountaineering. He was as accomplished at technical climbing in Europe as he was closer to home on the mild peaks. He was also the person least likely to tell someone all this. Never one to thump his chest, he simply loved being on the mountain. Along with Mike Coen, a fellow associate pastor at a local Christian church in Arvada, the late July climb marked their second-to-last Fourteener and my fourteenth.

The journey to Snowmass is twenty-two miles round trip. For most who attempt the peak, the distance necessitates a backpack loaded with overnight gear, nearly a third of my body weight, and several thousand feet of elevation gain to establish a base camp near Snowmass Lake. Frequent rises and falls over the initial eight miles, while keeping my inner core tight and crossing a 100-feet log jam over the roaring Snowmass creek, left me exhausted when we reached the lake and set up camp.

At sunrise, I took an upside-down photo of Hagerman Peak reflected on the lake's surface and snapped images around the valley. Common bluebells, Indian paintbrushes, and blue, white, red, and yellow representations of the state flower, the Columbine, created a garden-like effect around the lake's perimeter. In all the years of my quest, the photos that morning remain the most beautiful I have ever captured.

The morning's steep scree field forced us to take one giant step up and a half step slide back down for several hundred vertical feet. We worked our way across a large snowfield with a superb overview of the wilderness, crested the knife-edge ridge no wider than a man's shoe, and ascended to the class-three summit, the clouds, the dreamy photo. After a fun glissade down the snowfield and a steep descent, we rested for the next day's demanding hike to North Maroon Peak.

I arose from my tent the following morning to shake off the stiffness and stare at the striking crystal-blue canopy. Colorado's ten-thousand-foot skies are breathtaking. Unreal. The Buckskin Pass trail was all forest and flowers. We encountered a fellow hiker who offered to take a group photo—Mike in his maroon pants and a smile that was all eyes behind his glasses, Vince with his trademark floppy sun hat and leather shoelace cross around his neck, and me, the weakest link, resting on a rock.

North Maroon was uneventful until we encountered a series of class three and class four cliff bands and rock ledges. Mike reminded us to be a tripod—always three points of contact on the mountain. Glancing below at what we had ascended, we noticed clouds gathering. Experience told us time was not on our side. After four hours of brutal effort, we were at the final push to the top when the storm broke and barraged the summit with snow and freezing rain. The rocks glazed. This was Vince and Mike's *last* Fourteener, but the weather left us little choice but to turn around.

Our descent was slow. Achingly slow. The slippery rock required careful hand and foot-hold placements. We utilized a collective chatter to guide each other's best path. We reached our camp two hours later, but the day was far from done. We loaded our camping gear into our packs and hiked the eight miles back to the trailhead. At the restaurant on the way home, we devoured enough food to make a dent in the protein loss from three days of exertion, more than ten thousand vertical feet, and twenty-five miles of hiking—by far the most physical of my Fourteeners to that point.

In August, the three of us attempted North Maroon again, this time from the Aspen side. In only five miles, climbers gain over four thousand feet. The route is intricate, loose, vulnerable, and treacherous. The Maroon Bells have the second-highest number of deaths of any Fourteener.

After two thousand vertical feet, we transitioned to a bulging middle of the mountain—little more than a goat trail before the final ascent.

From above, someone yelled, "Rocks!"

I pressed myself to the mountain.

A rock not much smaller than my head plummeted beside me.

Vince and I shared a wide-eyed look.

"Let's keep our eyes peeled for who's above us," he advised.

The final one-thousand vertical feet required navigating a series of exposed gullies and ledges before finally reaching the ridge leading to the summit. Being part of what Mike and Vince had accomplished was a special moment.

This was the last time I climbed with them.

Vince went on to summit major mountains in South America and attempt Everest three times. In August 2008, ten years after Snowmass and North Maroon, Vince fell to his death on the Matterhorn in Switzerland.

On the drive to Vince's funeral, I passed a local private airport. The day was windy. A crow and a hawk soared side by side, completely unmoving, surfing air currents.

At the chapel, Mike greeted me. Projected on the wall for mourners was the photo on North Maroon that the stranger had taken—me, the weakest link, Mike with his eye smile, and Vince—all floppy hat and cross around his neck.

Surreal. Appropriate.

Vince died doing what he loved to do.

"My god, look at the carnage going on over there," I said to Darlene over the evening news.

For several years, I had been drawn to the plight of Northern Ireland and a terrible conflict known as *The Troubles*. Violence and death on the streets of Belfast and other smaller towns deeply affected me. Targeted assassinations and bombings by paramilitary groups took a terrible toll. Children were caught in the crossfire and ended up injured and dead.

It wasn't the Ireland I remembered.

In 1998, on a call with a minister friend in Virginia, I mentioned how much the sectarian violence in Northern Ireland disturbed me.

"I feel like it's happening to my family." I was at a loss to explain my inner turmoil regarding something happening four thousand miles away. "I want to do something, but I feel helpless."

"One of my parishioners here in Richmond has been hosting children through an organization called Project Children," he said. "I'll give you the New York phone number for the chairman of the organization. Might be worth a phone call."

Project Children originated around a dinner table in Greenwood Lake, New York. Denis Mulcahy, a bomb squad detective with the New York Police Department, along with friends and family who lamented the violence in their homeland, came up with an idea to sponsor children from the hardest-hit areas. The program's initial goal was to gift children a bit of the innocence that grenades and Saracen tanks had stolen.

The premise was simple: fly the children to America for an idyllic 6-week summer just as Marching Season—the series of Protestant marches celebrating an ancient victory over a Catholic king in 1690—began in earnest. The organization matched the children with host families who displayed healthy interpersonal relations—not necessarily between Protestants and Catholics, but that dynamic certainly came into play stateside. Unlike in Northern Ireland, where sectarian violence happens on a block-by-block basis and has a long history with forgotten motivations, the carefully curated slice of America selected as host families represented acceptance and diversity, where people of all nationalities, religions, affiliations, and belief systems could coexist in harmony.

I called Denis. Impressed by him and the project's vision, I took on the responsibility of securing quality host families for the summer and fundraising to fly four children from New York to Colorado. When I told Darlene what I had volunteered for, my whole body was base-parachute-level nerves. I should have discussed it with her first, but I'd been so impressed by Denis and not a little starstruck at the sphere of powerful influencers he had amassed in the name of peace in Ireland that I had closed my eyes and jumped. Would this be like Quandary's *Go have fun, dear?*

I needn't have worried. As always, Darlene understood me in an unprecedented way. She knew how much I cared for the children caught in the conflict and my heart for Ireland. Through my maternal heritage, I shared a connection, an affinity, for the innocents. Because of that, I likely paid closer attention to events in Ireland than most Americans, who were generationally and geographically far removed from the violence.

To me, the Irish dead might have been family.

It took me years to realize the dead *were* my family. I grieved the tragic loss of innocence and the children with no agency over their safety. A childhood reared in violence fundamentally distorts the human experience. I was an expert on that human experience. And that's what propelled me to involve myself deeply in Project Children.

Fundraising proved to be a challenge. I don't easily ask people for funds. I'm not comfortable parting people with their money. Darlene played a pivotal role in this aspect. She mobilized wives and mothers in a way that spotlighted Project Children as a family and community project, not just fragmented projects. Women and word-of-mouth are a powerful combination. As summers passed and more families engaged with Project Children, the growth of the Colorado contingent to Project Children was organic.

Timeline-wise, my Fourteener quest and my involvement with Project Children became so intertwined that they became doorways with no doors. Emotionally, the two journeys ran parallel as well. I was as invested in the Irish children and their host families as I was in summiting my next peak. The highs were life-affirming; the lows were life-altering.

Life, death, and all the beautiful messiness in between.

To understand the Irish children who came under my supervision, knowing their world is necessary.

Organized by The Orange Order, a group founded in 1795 during an earlier period of sectarian conflict to help preserve Protestantism in the United Kingdom, the march on Drumcree became the spark for regular violence each summer for hundreds of years. Beginning at the village of Loughgall, a few miles from Drumcree in County Armagh, the first marches were held on July 12, 1796, through Portadown, Lurgan, and nearby Waringstown. As a result, the area is seen as the birthplace of Protestant Orangeism. In July of that year, Reverend Devine held a Battle of the Boyne commemoration sermon at Drumcree Church. In his History of Ireland Volume I, published in 1809, historian Francis Plowden elaborated on what followed from Devine's sermon:

"[Reverend Devine] so worked up the minds of his audience, that upon retiring from service [...] they gave full scope to the anti-papistical zeal, with which he had inspired them; falling upon every Catholic they met, beating and bruising them without provocation or distinction, breaking the doors and windows of their houses, and murdering two unoffending Catholics in a bog."

What a bastard.

For over two hundred years, the Orangemen marched from the Lurgan town center to a Protestant church at the top of a hill called Drumcree, built upon the ruins of a former Catholic church bordered by Catholic housing estates. According to an account in 1835 by Armagh magistrate William Hancock (a Protestant), "The peaceable inhabitants of the parish of Drumcree have been insulted and outraged by large bodies of Orangemen parading the highways, playing party tunes, firing shots, and using the most opprobrious epithets they could invent." He added that the Orangemen go "a considerable distance out of their way" to pass a Catholic chapel on their march to Drumcree.

In 1968, peaceful marches took place to end discrimination against Catholics in the city of Derry (or Londonderry if you identified with the British side of things) and surrounding Northern Ireland towns. Complaints included job discrimination, housing allocation, and gerrymandering of local elections. The peace marches intended to raise awareness and reform the methods and misrepresentation of the Royal Ulster Constabulary (RUC), the police force whose ranks were over ninety percent Protestant and prone to excessive brutality against Catholics.

As the marches swelled and intensified, the RUC and Protestant paramilitaries engaged in brutal displays of force: beatings, bombings, shootings, and unprovoked attacks on citizens. British troops were brought in to keep the peace.

They never left.

Hunger strikes, or the *Troscad*, was an ancient Celtic practice that became a method of protest during this period. When someone felt wronged, they would go to the home of the person who had given injury and fast there until the guilty party made amends or, if need be, die by starvation. This was the ultimate way of lowering a person from a higher class. If the aggrieved were given justice, healing was possible. Bobby Sands, IRA member and leader of the ten Hunger Strikers who starved themselves to death in Long Kesh Prison in 1981, was famous for saying, "Our revenge will be the laughter of our children."

Over the subsequent three decades, the Provisional Irish Republican Army (IRA) and other Irish paramilitary groups targeted the British for overstaying their initial lukewarm welcome. Fighting intensified. By the late 1990s, nightly global news displayed the horrors of modern warfare on the streets of Belfast and reported the day's body counts. This new, violent era became known collectively as The Troubles, a wickedly polite way to define slaughter.

I followed news reports showing security forces entering Portadown, Northern Ireland, along with armored vehicles. By late June of 1998, in response to ten thousand Orangemen and Protestant loyalists gathering for the Drumcree march, approximately one thousand British troops and one thousand RUC officers were deployed. The British army had built a large barricade on the road linking the Protestant Drumcree Church to the Garvaghy Road and a nearby Catholic housing estate. A trench was constructed and lined with barbed wire through nearby fields to separate the two divided communities.

Tragically, the news became even more heart-wrenching. On July 13, 1998, three Catholic boys, ages seven, nine, and ten, were firebombed to death in their home in County Antrim by a Protestant paramilitary group called the UVF (Ulster Volunteer Force) simply because their Catholic mother was living with a Protestant man.

Could any sane person assume these boys had yet developed a religious identity to justify taking their lives in such a horrible way?

My dentist and one-time mountain companion, Mark Belford, was the first person I asked to host a child. He and his wife, Katie, were kind and loving souls, and they had two boys around the same age as the children assigned to me.

I excitedly explained Project Children to him and then joked, "I promise I won't try to get you up another mountain. Is this something you could do with me?"

"We're not churchgoers. Is that okay?"

"More than okay."

"Then yes, let's do it. We'll take a child of any faith. Our boys will enjoy having another brother for the summer."

To hear him say *brother* reaffirmed that my instincts to ask him were spot-on.

I matched the Belford family with Neil, a rugged young man of eleven from Omagh, a town in Northern Ireland. He was from a single-parent Protestant family and was unprepared for the size of a typical American house. Neil's first words when they brought him to their Boulder home: "How dya heat this fuckin place?"

On the day I added Mount Elbert to my list—August 15, 1998—I returned home to a call from Mark.

"Neil's mom just called. A massive car bomb went off in Omagh."

Young Neil's hometown.

I dropped my boots in the hallway. "His family okay?"

"Yeah, but there were children, Anthony. She said Neil almost always played on that street at that time of day. She was so upset I could barely understand her. She kept saying she was glad he was in America. That we'd saved his life."

A splinter group of the IRA (Irish Republican Army), known as the Real IRA, opposed the Good Friday Agreement that had been signed thirteen weeks earlier and wanted to demonstrate their insistence that the British leave Northern Ireland. They parked a stolen red Vauxhall Cavalier in front of a crowded clothes shop on Market Street and phoned cryptic and conflicting warnings into the local media and law enforcement, chronicling a thirty-minute countdown to detonation. In the confusion over which car on which street would detonate, the police evacuated innocent bystanders and encouraged them to gather around the red Cavalier.

A remote device triggered the five-hundred-pound bomb. Twenty-one lives were lost instantly. Three hundred people suffered injuries. Among the victims were Spanish students visiting nearby Buncrana and children from County Donegal.

It was the single deadliest attack during The Troubles.

The Irish children were to return home the following week.

The realization hung as heavy and rigid on my shoulders as a three-day pack. I didn't know what to say. Beyond wanting to keep me informed, as the local coordinator, I sensed Mark was looking for guidance on what to say or do.

The rest of the Project Children coordinators shared my helplessness. We hosted hundreds of children across the US and kept them safe. But with no peace for their families back home, would our cooperative efforts unravel when these kids returned to Northern Ireland's volatile climate?

"We should remind them how much we care about them. All the children."

"We want to pay to bring Neil back next year," Mark said. "We love him too much to risk not seeing him again."

For the next four years, they paid Project Children to facilitate Neil's return each summer. Though this was beyond the program's intent and scope, it was far from uncommon. Families who hosted often went all in emotionally. The Belfords so wanted to see the Irish lad succeed in life that they took steps to bring him permanently to America and even expressed a willingness to pay for his college.

✦

Beginning with Grays and Torreys that July Fourth, and throughout the summer and early fall, I summited eleven peaks, eight of them solo. These included Mount Massive, Pikes Peak, La Plata Peak, Mount Harvard, and Mount Columbia.

Feeling the itch to share the mountain with a climbing friend again, I reached out to Leaman. Daniel was a member of Vince and Mike's church. We met in late October to hike the nine miles to the summit of Mount Yale. Our abilities and pace were well-matched, except that he could talk non-stop going uphill, and I couldn't.

After the isolation of my solo runs, I was content to spend the hike in a pocket of listening.

With a clear day to enjoy the trail and compare our similarities in life's journey—raising a young family, juggling careers up against the same crazy Fourteener pursuit, and the places in Roanoke and Virginia Beach familiar to us both—we savored the best part of living in Colorado. The lower hike was warm enough to be in a t-shirt. We crossed two lively streams that sluiced around fallen logs and rocks, then gained five thousand feet in elevation through an upper basin with an ambitious pitch. We layered up to cross remnant snow fields and encountered Yale's notorious cold winds on the class-two ridge. The hike to a successful summit took us four hours.

We agreed to check another conquest off our list the following summer, but Mount Yale remained our only hike together. The following warm season proved so busy that I only added one peak to my quest. My religious interests shifted away from Daniel, Vince, and Mike's Faith Bible Church, and I met a new friend who became a significant hiking partner in my journey.

Two years after Yale, Daniel died during his descent on Capitol Peak.

Daniel had been a gift—not even for a season but for one day. Just one day. A blip in life. I was saddened but glazed. Compartmentalizing the tragedy meant that I could push on in my quest. It wasn't until I was on Capitol and stared down my own exit that Daniel's loss knocked the wind out of me.

I should have named my boots. Spoke to them when I hiked. Buried them.

Then again, giving them a persona beyond size twelve, Rocky brand might have been one crazy brain cell too far in my determination to finish my fifty-fifth peak in the pair I started.

They were Gore-Tex moccasins with traction, the most comfortable boots I had ever worn. Darlene gave them to me when I grew serious about hiking. They gripped wet rocks without slipping and shielded my bony ankles from injury.

Over my eighteen-year relationship with these boots, we disappointed each other. At times, I made false summits or didn't take them all the way due to weather or conditioning. Climbing is nothing if not unpredictable. Sometimes, we both needed to be fixed. Resoling them three times no longer made them waterproof. I frontloaded my goals list with easy peaks. More challenging peaks came when the boots had grown tired. But we kept each other. They became a point of conversation when my introversion failed me. They projected loyalty. They were flawed, and so was I. We both understood what it meant to fall short but step forward anyway.

"The patches look like faces," my local shoemaker once told me. While his wife stitched wedding gowns and his children played in the back of his shop, the cobbler stretched new material over the armored toes and shaped fresh soles with a coarse-grit sander.

Each time I returned from a summit, Darlene reminded me to stash the boots in the basement. The boots no longer breathed well with all the patching and other repairs. Overheated feet led to wicked smells, but I didn't want to make the change.

At twenty-two peaks in, we were committed to each other to the end.

The void of healthy, formidable figures initially pushed me toward organized religion. I moved through religious doctrines like a holy buffet—first, Irish Catholic, then Methodist, evangelical Christian, Messianic, and psionic and informal Judaism. I was searching for the wise man—and I use the term *man* loosely. I have always been open to genderless spirituality. Even one, just one, figure in the present or in the folklore of faith, who held satisfactory answers to questions I had yet to ask.

It never quite worked out.

Carl Faircloth was a notable exception.

Carl introduced me to Darlene, so there was that win. He had already captured my favor.

But there is something to be said for finding a mentor in your twenties when your most obvious bloodline guides and weekend-morning orators have failed you. It's a magnetism, an enlightening to how it always should have been, and a hunger to devour all you have missed.

Less idolatry. More relief.

Before Carl, there were others: a fifth-grade teacher during our brief stint in Maine who recognized my interest in books and fed me everything she could get her hands on, and middle school and high school teachers in Virginia who inspired and reinforced the good they saw in me. These educators were doing their jobs; they were outstanding at it. Someone noticing and taking an interest beyond obligation is, however, a special kind of nurturing.

Though he was more of the age of an older brother, Carl seemed to move through life already seasoned. He was a boss for a time, a friend longer than obligation, and a sounding board with a tremendous capacity for listening. He modeled a rapport with people I carried into every job. At many of my life's crossroads—changing jobs, changing careers, deciding to marry—I called him.

I did not set out to become a Carl. I made no deliberate efforts to become a wise man to anyone. I held no satisfactory answers. And yet, for the Project Children kids we welcomed to Colorado and into our home, I aimed to go beyond obligation. I listened to their stories and told some of my own. They had parents at home, so it was more important to me to provide them with an opportunity to relax and have fun. In the same way the educators in Maine and Virginia found something noteworthy in me, I complimented the Irish children in ways that approximated positive life directions. As young as they were, these children did not simply fly over to America with a chip on their veneer and a need for a vacation. Project Children participants arrived motivated and focused on their life's journeys in a way that outpaced their ages. They were extraordinary and inspiring.

They became my wise figures.

Mount Lindsey 14,042'

Chapter Five

Shortly after two high school students strapped themselves with nine millimeters, twelve-gauge shotguns, and backpacks full of homemade bombs, entered Columbine High School in Littleton, Colorado, and murdered thirteen people, I met Colorado's governor, Bill Owens. I wanted to show him that hosting children from war-torn Northern Ireland for a summer taught them that the rest of the world was non-violent.

The irony gutted me.

Like many parents from Colorado—all over the country, really—a divide surfaced in my innocence of parenthood. Before Columbine and after Columbine. My daughters were still elementary aged, but like so many others, the mantra *It could have been my child* played inside me like a guilt-ridden refrain in a song none of us asked to hear. Indeed, that was also the case for thousands of families in Northern Ireland who lived at the epicenter of violence and looked to a new program to get their children out of harm's way—if only for six weeks.

The night of the Columbine massacre, I had a dream. One of the female students waved to a crowd from a horse-drawn carriage. She smiled, surrounded by flowers. It seemed like I was watching a wedding, and then everything turned sad as the carriage arrived at the cemetery.

I awoke, shaken.

The vision was so vivid. I drove to the school and visited the many memorials throughout the parking lot. One deeply touched me: the first student killed. Her car was completely buried in flowers.

Not a month before the shooting, I had visited Denis Mulcahy at his home in Greenwood Lake, New York, so I could comb through the dossiers of the children being placed on the list to come from Ireland. I had committed to bringing fourteen children to Colorado, the most I would ever host for a summer. I wanted to find kids living in the most difficult circumstances. I mistakenly believed that Catholic children had struggled the most with single-parent homes, relatives being shot by paramilitaries, and living in public housing. I found six Protestant kids I wanted to bring to Colorado who had it bad in Belfast and Derry. With the nine Catholic kids I had selected, it would be an excellent opportunity to build bridges.

After Columbine, what would the Irish parents think?

Would they be reluctant to send their children to America? To Colorado, specifically? This no longer seemed like the Colorado I was familiar with. *My* Colorado was boundless and tranquil and enlightened. What kind of peaceful bridges happened over rivers of chaos perpetuated by children with access to guns? Was all hope in a safe harbor of what should be places of peace—home, school, playgrounds—gone forever?

At the time, Columbine High School was the worst mass school shooting in U.S. history. I couldn't fathom the seed of insanity being sown in our country that we would become so barbaric on many more occasions.

In Ireland, sectarian violence is front and center. Summers were rife with conflict. Violence was carried out by those with the means and access to weapons of harm. But in a zero-gun society, few had access to those means and weapons, certainly not children. There is radical honesty in a culture that puts it out front and has forgotten how to apologize about it.

It doesn't make the aggression better, just different.

Domestically, however, Columbine shifted the polarity. Americans had not yet owned our violence. Though our history was rife with inward atrocities at our underbelly, the larger world had always painted our society with a broad brush of the underdog good guys that looked like farmer revolutionaries or figureheads of righteous vigilantes like the Lone Ranger or Batman or valiant protestors. Now, our children were paying the toll for our brutal adherence to personal freedoms at the expense of our neighbors.

And it has. not. stopped.

The 1975 America in which Project Children was born is not 1999s or 2020s America. Project Children could not happen today. The violence is here.

America once held hope.

The truth hurts.

Coach Taylor was a blip on my high school radar. His existence barely registered with me. He was every bit a typical wrestling coach—a hulking presence with little to impress rolling off his tongue. It didn't even occur to me that he might read but for the morning edition of the local paper he brought to gym class one day.

For marginalized kids, the boy's locker room in high school is a tenth circle of Dante's *Inferno*: the outer ring of a frozen wasteland where the pale and gaunt inwardly shiver and change into too-short shorts like their clothes might spontaneously combust, and the inner flaming River Clique, where egotistical pirates pillage the spoils of decent souls who drown in the social currents. I had perfected the art of being first to change clothes and assemble for class—a tolerable sort of purgatory that involved awkward conversations with the adult teachers and sometimes helping to set up the day's equipment.

We had just finished moving mats into place when Coach Taylor stretched tall. His stare lingered on me.

"Saw you on the front page this morning," he said, hands propped on his hips, stance wide—all pirate.

I stared at the bullseye florescent lights, the flags of bygone eras of sports victories, anywhere but directly at him. The article had been folded on my breakfast table. Mom had circled my name with a ballpoint pen, so proud. Like I was more than just a decent runner, a middleman of sorts, on a cross-country running team that had become Eastern District Champions in Virginia. The accompanying color photo had captured a handful of us running on the track toward the camera. I looked uncharacteristically happy in that snapshot.

I nodded, unsure how to respond.

Coach Taylor moved closer.

The bright, clinical lights seemed to dim.

"Finally good at something, eh?"

My cheeks flamed. Spontaneously combusting right there would have been preferable to standing in the limelight of what was my proudest accomplishment to date, reduced to nothing.

No one heard him, which magnified the sentiment. *I see through you. You're nothing.*

I was physically built for little more than being a windchime in a strong gale. No baseball. No basketball. Certainly not wrestling. The currency of being aerodynamic held no value for him.

Coach Taylor was no different than those who occupied the locker room.

When I turned eighteen, I enrolled in local *wing chun* classes. This South China specialty of kung fu is all about the efficiency and simultaneity of attacking and defending. No movement is wasted. It's close-quarters resistance with rapid-fire punches and hand-to-hand combat. I practiced for two years, enough to build my reflexes and confidence a bit, yet my body stature changed little.

Years later, into my late twenties, inside a dealership-type workplace environment with an assembled audience, a repair guy tried to kick me in the butt. Before my conscious mind registered what was happening, an overt act of bullying, my reflexes had me blocking his leg.

He yelped like a bitch and recoiled. His minions drifted away, unimpressed.

Another time, shortly after Darlene and I began dating, she agreed to a camping and seventeen-mile canoeing trip down the Rappahannock River with some coworkers we had in common. Canoeing in sixteen-foot Old Town canoes, I was firmly in my element. Our mutual boss was Johnny Hobbs, a football scholarship recipient at Virginia Military Institute. At over two hundred and fifty pounds, he was every bit Coach Taylor: an inflated sense of bodily presence, little to impress off the tongue. We had stopped at a convenience store to grab snacks, and Johnny lunged at me. My brain failed to process that he was joking around, and I forgot he was my boss. Wing Chun kicked in, and I had my elbow to his throat before he could blink.

I cannot say what Darlene must have thought at that moment. I was a set of whip-thin nun chucks unfolding at lightning speed over a gesture that was supposed to be playful. I was the lead oarsman in Frances Anne Hopkins' 1897 painting *Shooting the Rapids,* except when I wasn't. She did not yet know the earlier years of intimidation and the two years of finally learning to stand up for myself that had primed me for such overreaction.

My vessel was not populated with romanticized fur traders and prestigious land governors of Canada's settlement era; my vessel carried the grizzled depictions of family members traumatized by the remnants of war, mental illness, and alcoholism.

The most potent bullies of all.

I owned a 1980 baby blue luxury Colony Park station wagon with faux wood grain panels. Electric leather seats. Eighteen feet long and 302 cubic inches of V-8 power, the car glided down the road like a parade float. I loved that damned car. Well past the time it was an amusing conversation piece for its doppelganger in the movie *National Lampoon's Vacation,* I was convinced the wagon was the ultimate wingman on my Fourteener quest.

For mountains at a significant distance from home, I often folded down the wagon's back seat and stretched out my six-foot-two frame inside a sleeping bag for an overnight. Tents were messy and time-consuming, and I was impatient. Gerry Roach's guidebook detailed where to start odometer measurements for remote road markers and forest turn-offs. His notes also described how far into the route rugged terrain began and how far certain classes of vehicles could go. He'd classify access points on certain roads as *not passable for most passenger vehicles.*

And I'd think: *I'm good. We're good.*

Mercury may have marketed the vehicle as the perfect family wagon; to me, it was a rugged, go-anywhere all-terrain vehicle.

Well, almost anywhere.

That Fourth of July weekend, I set out for Mount Lindsey in the Sangre de Cristo Mountain range. Near the Huerfano River starting point, I pulled over on the side of the forest road and crashed for the night.

Along the trail to Mount Lindsey the next day, I met Wayne McClelland.

Wayne was a bit less polished than my other Fourteener partners. With a thick black headband holding his untamed hair back from his face, dark shades, and cutoff jeans as his top climbing layer, he looked like he'd be more at home fronting a Rolling Stones cover band than fronting the Sunday sermons of my previous companions.

At the trailhead, we left for Lindsey at the same time. He expressed that he did better with a buddy. I was happy for the company.

Wayne was chatty. It wasn't long before he said, "Saw you coming up the road yesterday with that station wagon, man. Couldn't believe you got as far as you did. Even with my Subaru, I didn't feel I could make it up as far as you did. Some people camping near me thought you were nuts."

His boldness made me laugh. "Yeah. Sometimes I think I'm in a tank."

On the ascent, we discovered that we had a similar hiking style. We crossed streams, entered a rubble filled chute, and eased from gulleys into open basins. The sun blasted our faces on our route toward the saddle ridge. We navigated past the namesake rock formation of one of the thirteen thousand-foot false summits, The Iron Nipple, and picked our way through The Crux, a high class-three ridge requiring three safety touchpoints.

At Lindsey's peak marker, we congratulated ourselves.

Wayne and I descended with an easy banter that I rarely felt with most people. By the time we reached our vehicles at the trailhead, we were reluctant to leave our companionship. We drove to a tavern in a small town nearby and had a beer. Exchanging phone numbers became a must. Wayne had bumped right up against the possibility that I was, in fact, nuts, as the other campers had proclaimed, but he had still spent the day with me. That meant he was likely nuts too. I was excited that some of my Fourteeners might be shared with my new friend.

Mount Lindsey marked peak twenty-four for me. Though Lindsey was the only mountain I made time for that summer due to work and my newly minted involvement with Project Children, I was optimistic about my progress toward the end goal.

Sadly, modern-day climbers on Fourteener quests faced recent legal and political challenges regarding Lindsey and some of the other most coveted peaks, such as Lincoln and Democrat, not located on public lands.

Owners whose land held prominent peaks began to close access to climbers, citing litigation concerns. In prior years, legal precedents had been set regarding similar lands where people were injured and successfully sued a private entity. The Colorado legislature's failure to clarify, protect, and indemnify private landowners under a proper recreational use law left them little choice but to classify anyone on their property as a trespasser.

In my estimation, that makes the sue-happy people, their lawyers going after deep pockets, and the state's elected officials, who spent years stumbling around a more permanent solution to free the peaks for everyone to enjoy, the ones who are nuts.

I have three brothers.

One is missing the front temporal lobe of his brain. One followed my father into the dark *isms* of life. And one, the youngest of us all, circled back around and became my hero.

Men's relationships are complex. To the core of our DNA, we are superficial, antagonistic, and self-serving creatures. Add to that a dysfunctional and unhealthy childhood environment filled with geographical upheaval, generational trauma, and not a little malt whiskey from the old country, and you have a blended concoction that leads to heartache.

But boys do not originate in heartache.

The four of us boys were all we had, once.

Early on, Kevin and I were close in age and proximity. He was a year younger—reserved, laid back. We found commonality on playgrounds and around kids our age in the American neighborhoods where we were perpetually the new kids with the weird accents. Philly, Jersey, back to England, then Florida, Maine, and finally Virginia— we squirmed through them all. Kevin and I also shared a room. Our teenage years marked a departure of interests. I climbed out the window at night to join friends and run the streets, and Kevin wanted to stay in bed. Naturally, we grew apart.

Douglas and Curtis shared the other bedroom down the hall. Doug was one of my first bullies, but Curtis got the worst of his older brother's wrath. Doug was more verbal about life's displeasure than most. His argumentative nature made him a physical target for my father. As the saying goes, shit rolls downhill. Doug was the first to tap into the house's liquor stash and developed drug and alcohol addiction at a young age. We did not know until Doug reached his late teens, sometime before he went away to college, that the portion of his brain that processes emotions and controls impulses didn't exist. Until these medical epiphanies, the family operated on the assumption that Doug was difficult because he chose to be, and his near-genius intellect would eventually pull him out of his problematic behaviors.

Of course, the most formidable role model in Doug's life—in all our lives—the same-sex parent—wasn't exactly free of problematic behaviors. It was hard to fight the bullies down the street and at school when the most dreadful ones lived under the same roof. The Massey boys entered the real world believing everyone was an adversary, cursing like sailors, and reacting to an extreme. Strength meant endurance. Best your brother got it than you.

Curtis and I grew up as strangers. We didn't connect emotionally.

Raising four boys, all born within five years of each other, while my father was gone much of the time on annual six-month deployments meant Mom carried out most of the parenting duties. She was a tired but capable disciplinarian who did the best she could. It's difficult to say if she'd had the means and support that she would have freed herself and us from the abuse. I have no knowledge of what form of discipline my maternal grandfather imposed on his five children in Ireland. I want to think that her worth was shaped more by my grandmother, especially if Mom's father was largely gone in spirit and emotionally vacant. Generationally and culturally, I can't help but think she accepted that how we lived was simply the way it had always been. Financially, raising four boys alone would have been a daunting prospect. Escaping back to her home in Dublin just wasn't possible. Her only option was to endure and survive. So, like us, she threaded herself through his moods and relished his absence.

As for my father, reestablishing discipline when he was home was paramount to him. We boys sometimes asked, "Dad, when are you leaving again?" Physical attacks on Mom and drunken episodes marked his stretches of family time. We all grew to fear him. In the 1960s and 70s, there was no socially accepted help for mental or emotional stress. When it came to the darkness within, men bottled the pressure. Once it became too much, the cork exploded, usually on those closest to you.

Group beatings were a thing. Our brotherly connection had the potential to lean into a fierce, protective trauma bond where loyalties to each other surpassed whatever Dad did to us. Sadly, even our brotherhood was not a refuge. The four of us navigated violence in separate silos of pain the best we knew how and split from the family home as soon as we could.

Years later, a dear friend published a book about Adolf Hitler. In the book, he describes Adolf's early childhood and how his father took great pleasure in beating his son. Initially, Adolf cried, but at eleven, he resolved never to shed another tear. After thirty-two lashes, his father stopped. Although Adolf was never beaten by his father again, the damage was done. Though I could never feel compassion toward the madman he became, I understood the origins of such a horrific outcome.

Every day in life becomes an intentional choice *not* to become everything you have known. I was determined that my daughters would see a father committed to their emotional and physical well-being, that they would enjoy a level of financial autonomy my mother never had, and that they'd never be dependent on a man.

But intentional choice doesn't always equate to mastery. I hold abundant love and intent for them but often do not know how to express it outwardly. I originated in heartache, but I will not depart in heartache.

Dad taking his boys on road trips to Civil War battlefields were glimmers inside my core childhood memories. From our Virginia home, we'd set out with a packed car and the breeze whipping through the windows. In places like Fredericksburg and Gettysburg, it was about looking around the town, locating the memorials, running through peach orchards, or mowing through greasy roadside hamburgers. History's gravity was lost on me because I was so young.

As I grew older and absorbed the true nature of the Confederacy's platform, I viewed these road trips quite differently. I came to understand that Dad made a hobby of visiting battlefields because his views aligned with the South's ideology—the complex and brutal effort to uphold their institutions, the ferocity with which Southern sympathizers touted freedom to the exclusion of the human rights of others. While I read the etchings on the stones, all that death so that people could own another human being, Dad was likely reading the same memorial and thinking *Fuckin Yankees, tellin' others what to do*. His darkness permeated all the isms: racism, sexism, chauvinism, egoism. Rural Virginia was fertile ground to plant his shadows and watch them bear spoiled fruit.

Sadly, some of his sons ate of that fruit.

With only abuse bonds to hold us, his sons went our estranged ways.

Curtis's healing came from being a firefighter, serving others, and being among an undeniably healthier brotherhood. I cannot speak to Kevin and Doug's healing. I hope the peach orchards and roadside hamburgers were enough to help them remember that they once had a nearly invisible and forgettable brother who wished things had turned out differently.

Healing, for me, came in nature.

My Fourteener quest was rooted, perhaps, in the same demons that drove an angry, alcoholic military veteran through the tangle of mental illness, but it didn't remain that way. Though I was angrier then, I didn't strike out after every Colorado Fourteener to die. Unlike my father, I could not hold darkness as my companion. I climbed to escape his phantom.

For the most part, I did.

I hoarded life's deviations and kept my accomplishments a secret, lest sharing them gave away their magic.

At some point, I realized I was in an aging body, and time was no equalizer. Starting a mission of this physicality in my forties left me restless in my skin. Because I did not climb on ice, the season of accomplishment occupied a narrow window in Colorado's high country. Despite my progress, twenty-three peaks into my goal, part of me believed I would not see the summit of all fifty-five. And so, I sought a different trail, an alternate method of escape that allowed me to chase magic.

I found that magic in Ireland, not on a dewy spring morning in Connemara where the sky reflects the water, or the run-down picturesque countryside houses of bygone eras, or the Dublin of my mother's youth, but on the bloody streets of Belfast at the tail end of a violent three-decades sectarian conflict between loyalist Protestants and Roman Catholic nationalists.

I found that magic in the children of Project Children—a way to right childhood for us all.

Fourteen miles down the road, fourteen hundred miles across the Atlantic.

Such indiscriminate carnage.

At the closing of summer 1999, the governor of Colorado, Bill Owens, and his staff warmly welcomed Project Children participants to his office. The Irish kids made a memorable impression. Weeks later, Governor Owens traveled to Northern Ireland for the anniversary of the Omagh bombing as a way of expressing solidarity for the many victims associated with our respective tragedies. During his visit, he presented $50,000 to the Omagh Bomb Appeal Fund to help the families of the bomb victims. Afterward, he said, "They've given me some advice which I'll keep private and pass on to families in Colorado. They've been through this for the past eleven months, and we are just starting down that journey." The father of one of the bomb victims, Michael Gallagher, said: "When we first hear about tragedies, we have a certain amount of empathy for the people who are involved. Being able to physically hold somebody's hand and say you're sorry can do more than just words on paper." Governor Owens spoke to other bereaved and injured people, including seventeen-year-old Clare Gallagher, who was blinded in the Omagh explosion. I was proud of Colorado, the people, the media, and its leaders for showing compassion beyond our borders. Pain, mourning, and loss become more bearable when shared with others.

Columbine brought about an urgency in me. I struggled to comprehend this level of hatred. To set aside my anxiety over violence I could not control, I redoubled my efforts to bring even more Irish children to Colorado the following year. The numbered toll of The Troubles is staggering: 3,500 dead, 50,000 injured. Children and innocents accounted for much of the losses. Three decades of sectarian violence irreversibly impacted one in every six citizens of Northern Ireland.

But the polarity shift of the past twenty-five years is not lost on me.

America—especially the America we are asking children to live in—is existence without grace. There are good times, but the adults in society imprint our toxicity and then ask our children to grow up without emotional baggage and hate. We live in enlightened times yet treat our purest and most vulnerable like second-class citizens. We plant shadows and are surprised the fruit that grows is spoiled. There is an injustice to this that rivals the violence in Northern Ireland during The Troubles. Sectarian violence hides behind history and leans into the notion that it's the way it's always been.

What excuse do Americans hide behind?

Project Children, as it existed, would not happen today. Irish families who wanted their children out of harm's way would not send their sons and daughters to America.

Then, they were shooting at each other.

Now, we are shooting at us.

Mount Antero 14,269' | Tabegauche Peak 14,155' |
Mount Shavano 14,229' | Mount of the Holy Cross 14,005' |
Huron Peak 14,003' | Pyramid Peak 14,018'

Chapter Six

Six years into the quest

My friend Harry tried to sell Jesus to the guy next to us on the quad chairlift. Knowing he had a captive audience for about five minutes, Harry became a leaflet with a pulse.

"You know, I have a ski buddy who helps me float on the snow," Harry said. "He gives me the wisdom to make good turns on the slopes and good turns in life. His name is Jesus Christ."

Jesus Christ. I rolled my eyes at the passing scenery.

The lift's safety bar was down. Escape for Harry's captive two-man audience wasn't possible. During the shuddering ride up the mountain, the guy endured what Harry called *soul deposits* to draw from the heavenly bank account.

As the hum of the arrival station grew louder, I clicked my skis together in anticipation.

Harry ended his alpine sermon at the chairlift exit with, "God bless you!"

The poor guy grunted out a hurried mumble of thanks, then took a stab at qualifying for the Olympics—the fastest start time ever recorded.

Harry's style of spreading Christianity's message wasn't my style. At one time, our beliefs coincided, but I realized everyone had to find their way. The term God wrestler didn't mean you had to take down the person across from you and pin them into believing.

I tried to forget that, at one time, Harry financed his hunger for epic turns on the slopes of France and Austria by selling drugs. People change. His newfound passion for Christianity permitted only the craving for the natural snow high of black diamond runs from sunup to sundown.

Harry once worked with his father in the undertaking business in Catskill, New York. He drove a long black hearse with a bumper sticker that read *Don't wait until one of these takes you to church.* I was drawn to his contradictions—a thrill-seeker who reigned it in enough to minister the Gospel. Someone who valued the air filling his lungs but charged down terrain that might snatch that same air at any moment. Someone who claimed to have found the answer to eternity enough to advise others, yet he, like so many of us, got caught up in the God machine that was a mega-church in Virginia Beach.

Later, I called it *The Deal*.

There was always a new deal or way to raise money at the mega-church. The leaders baffled me. Millionaire-style life. Denigrating others' beliefs. Prophesizing to couples going through divorce that they were at risk of going to Hell. Tearing out chunks of the Bible at the pulpit for shock value, only to later reveal that the destroyed copy was the Book of Mormon.

I emerged from the ordeal with a valuable life truth. The ones who speak loudest and most have the least to say about it all—organized religion, faith, spirituality.

The mid-October Indian summer of 1999 made me itch for my hiking boots. On the back end of a busy few months that included the lingering darkness of the Columbine tragedy, facilitating a perfect summer for fourteen children from Northern Ireland, and meeting the governor, I craved something profound.

A pair of Fourteeners on my list held the promise of something transcendent. Named after a band of the Ute Indian tribe, Mount Tabeguache translated to *people living on the warm side of the mountain.* Mount Shavano was named after a chief known for keeping the peace between his people and the settlers moving into the Arkansas River Valley in the mid-1800s. Mount Shavano is also known for its snow field, which presents the Angel of Shavano when the winter snows melt.

According to legend, a drought once took hold in the valley. A Native American princess went to the foot of the mountain to pray to the gods and weep for her people. One day, the God of Plenty answered her prayers. He beckoned to her, and she sacrificed herself so her people could live. Every year, the Princess—the Angel of Shavano—reappears and weeps once more for her people. Her tears, the melting snow, nourish the land below and make it fertile.

I needed to see that angel.

At the Angel of Shavano campground, six miles from the turn-off to the national forest, the road became rough. In winter, Chafee County Road 240 is plowed to the Angel of Shavano Campground but not beyond. It wasn't yet winter, so I felt confident I could drive my battle-axe family wagon within reach of the trailhead. After clocking in a fifty-hour workweek and driving five hours to knock out two mountains at once, my superhero-caliber confidence knew no bounds. It was nearly midnight when I pulled my car to the side of the road, climbed in the back, and stretched out in my sleeping bag.

At 5:30 the next morning, my internal alarm woke me. I yawned and climbed behind the steering wheel to begin the final drive to the Jennings Creek Trailhead. Guessing it was only a few miles further, I was confident I'd make the turnoff by sunrise. I rounded a bend in the rising road.

My headlights illuminated a slope of solid ice.

Unwilling to waste my efforts to get there, I reversed back down the mountain road a bit to get a running start, then punched the accelerator to a quick ten miles per hour. When my tires hit the ice, I added gas pressure for momentum.

I almost made it to the top.

Almost.

Traction beneath the tires disappeared.

A trapdoor opened in my stomach.

My forward momentum stalled. The wagon slid backward at first, ever so slowly, then increasingly faster.

Adrenaline shot through me and raced my pulse. I pumped the brakes to slow my descent. Pines and firs blurred past the windows. I want to say at that moment that I had the presence of mind to bail, to breathe past my locked-up chest and give my brain a fighting chance at a coherent thought—or, at the very least, to witness important events in my life like some fast-forward, grandiose projection against the ice-crusted windshield.

None of those things happened.

The wagon came to a crunching halt, two tires on the mountain and two tires off. Trees on the opposite side loomed above my window. My heart had lodged itself between my tonsils. It took several minutes to regain my composure, slow my heart rate, and return to a manageable state of panic.

Grateful to be alive, I considered my next move. There was no way I was getting out of the predicament without help. My phone carried a signal, so I dialed 911. The State Patrol answered. The dispatcher said they would send an officer to assist me immediately.

I delicately shifted the transmission into park and popped open the door. The road was still beneath me, close enough to reach out and touch. No part of the car or I moved. Of my two options—stay still, stay warmer, and wait for help or risk the car's stability by crawling out and inviting frostbite—I opted to remain inside.

Sitting in the driver's seat, shivering from the cold and my frayed nerves, waiting for sunrise, I replayed the mental reel of almost making it to the crest and the sensation of sliding backward.

I berated myself. What the hell had inspired me to make such a crazy decision? Even if I had skated the wagon to the trailhead at the top, I still would have had to drive down the sheet of ice to go home. Not wanting to add a few miles to my hike had nearly killed me.

Around seven in the morning, as daylight strengthened, a state trooper arrived.

"I assume you're Mr. Massey? Looks like you're in a bind." He gave the wagon a once-over study. "How did this happen?"

"I thought I could drive up that slip of ice. Seeing it in the daylight, I realize it wasn't a smart choice."

"You're shaking. Let's get you in my car. I'll call in some help."

He radioed for a tow truck and let me warm up in his car until it arrived. The wagon's driver-side door was dented from sliding sideways over small aspen trees; otherwise, the car didn't look too damaged. The officer didn't scold me. Perhaps he was accustomed to responding to the consequences of people operating at my level of stupidity.

The officer attempted polite conversation. "Usually, when I get this kind of call, the people haven't survived." He gripped the front of his vest, somewhere warm to rest his hands, and glanced around. The pause stretched long before he added, "And they're usually in four-wheel drive vehicles, not passenger cars."

He said *passenger cars,* but I heard, *damn, what is this piece of shit?*

When the tow truck arrived, the trooper bid me farewell. The plan to rescue the car involved a steel cable clipped to the wagon's undercarriage, a hydraulic winch, and a pulley system rigged around a sturdy pine tree across the road. As the operator turned on the winch and started to pull, the cable snapped.

"Car's on too steep an incline to pull it up while it's in park," said the tow truck driver.

I reached through the driver's side window and moved the column shift to neutral.

The gear shift was the only thing holding the car in place. Unfortunately, I remembered that detail a half-second too late.

Before I could get my head out of the window, the wagon shot down the slope and knocked me down. I fell to the ground. Front tire treads barely cleared my head.

A curse bomb from the tow driver skated to my eardrums.

The baby blue luxury Colony Park smashed into a pine tree half the width of its tailgate.

In the ensuing silence, I turned to granite—my posture, my limbs. Even my lungs found no room to expand. Everything but my brain solidified. My ride was more than a station wagon with faux wood panels; it connected me to my quest. A quest I hadn't yet finished.

I worked my way down the slope to survey the damage. Gasoline smell was potent.

Shattered back window.

Crushed tailgate.

Punctured fuel tank.

Nonplussed, clearly recalibrated from his f-bomb, the tow truck driver said, "This time, I'll use two steel cables. I'm sure that'll do it." He worked his cables, chains, and gears until the wagon surfaced like a bowhead whale in Arctic waters.

I climbed behind the wheel to start the car and drive it up onto the tow truck bed, unmindful that one stray spark might ignite a firestorm. It didn't start. The tow truck driver hooked a cable under the bumper and pulled it onto the truck bed. After a short, leaky drive to a salvage yard in Buena Vista, two bolts, and one neoprene rubber patch for the gas tank, I started the three-hour drive home. The wagon, my steel wingman, was no longer the seductive beast it had once been. The day's events left me with two realizations.

My car was not a snowcat.

And I was damned lucky to be alive.

I should have surrendered the wagon then. After scoring a wood grain tailgate in Worland, Wyoming, and replacing the fuel tank, I drove the wagon another fifty thousand miles. Like the boots, I valued badges of honor more than things untouched. The driver's side door dent reminded me I had, and would probably always, sacrifice good judgment in my desire to summit fifty-five peaks.

My faith journey is an alpine gondola ride.

A gondola is a continuous system that circulates waystations—nexuses of organized movement and processes that leave travelers no choice but to get off and look around. At the first station, the most burdensome spot from an engineering standpoint, the gondola turns tightly on its steel wire cables. This was the birth station of my Irish Catholic roots—the rituals, the confessions, the one-church-one-answer doctrine. As far back as boyhood, standing beside that pond in England, I sought to understand my consciousness. Why do we have one? What, exactly, is consciousness? What can we make of our imperfect inner selves when held up against an idealized, God-like entity? Is God largely a construct of man? And yet, Catholicism leaves little permission for such questions.

Subsequent forays into other organized religions were waystations where I became an honest investigator—embracing, practicing, and chasing the right angles to properly define and compartmentalize truths that made sense for my path. My Protestant journey came in many flavors. The image of God shifted based on the presenter. Through one of the children I sponsored, I learned that Irish Protestants were taught that Catholics had little horns under their hair.

Invariably, I'd decide a particular religion wasn't the right fit. Then, I'd move to the next station, suspended by a cable, where I'd flex and shift with the pressure.

For now, I have exited the ride. I detached myself from all organized religions, believing them to be nothing but ineffectual dishonesty, little more than a political system wrapped in an ancient shroud that aimed for control, inherently flawed and infinitely corruptible. For now, my spiritual sweet spot is sweat on my brow with a breathless view in all directions.

The wilderness helps me contemplate how to make my life happier and more meaningful. In nature, I have experienced places that enchant and carry resonance like no other, time that collapses, chance encounters that defy rational cause and effect, and heights that are nothing less than mystical with an indescribable frequency. Being outdoors, beyond the touch of anything man created, felt natural as if this was how it was always meant to be, but somehow humankind lost sight of that. Quiet moments alone on the trail, reaching summits, then beginning arduous descents created a full circle, renewing experience as close to godly as I could find.

Inside a belief system that makes room for the possibility of an afterlife, a sense of confidence takes hold. In whatever framework you find yourself, in theory, you can nestle into a sort of boundless comfort of that certainty, so long as you adhere to expectations. But those questions by the pond never left me, and I moved through all the conventional faith systems to arrive at a perspective that we are finite creatures in our consciousness. It's no longer boundless, so best not take it for granted. I embrace moments and breathe through my state of being wherever I find myself, physically and mentally and emotionally.

Brushes with death brought me closer than ever to a deep and nourishing understanding of my place in this world. I came to appreciate my near-death encounters as not a cheat of death and the afterlife but encouragement to move ahead. I felt deeply appreciated, as if the universe or whatever moves and evolves us said, *stick around awhile, maybe talk to a few others and help them.*

Maybe the final answer is not for us to know but merely to experience.

At the cable loop's opposite end is my death station. I cannot say where I will be spiritually, but it will result from many studies, a gradual ascent of awareness, and a general satisfaction that any one waystation isn't the answer. At least, not my answer.

While the world grieved the September 11, 2001, terrorist attacks on the World Trade Center in New York and Washington D.C., another example of religious hatred played out at a small Catholic girls' school in Ardoyne, North Belfast.

Ardoyne was an economically depressed area made up of predominantly Catholic families. Holy Cross Girls Primary School was in a Protestant area, separated by a 20-foot-high wall that was part of the *Peace Line*. Throughout the summer, tensions escalated. Protestants and Catholics believed they were being pushed out of their homes by the other side, which led to increasingly isolated neighborhoods. Access to the school required the girls, ages four to eleven, to walk through the Protestant area.

On their daily walk to school, these girls endured a bombardment of balloons filled with urine, dog excrement in paper bags, fireworks tossed at their feet, pornographic pictures held out for them to see, and shrill whistles and horns blown in their ears as they passed protestors.

Father Aiden Troy, a priest at the school, lost count of the death threats against him. He did his best to lead the girls to school daily and model strength and calm. At the end of the first week of protests, a little girl handed him a bag with two sweets inside—one for him and one for the second priest at the school. Another girl told Father Troy that she had seen people shouting in his face on television. She motioned for him to come close, took his face in her tiny hands, and stroked his cheeks as she had done to his likeness through the screen.

Three months later tensions eased. More than half the girls went into counseling. Father Troy shared that a man called him to apologize for spitting directly in his face during the protests. The caller added that he had, on occasion, seriously considered plowing into the priest with his car as he walked alone on the street. Father Troy asked the man why he called to tell him such things. The man had seen the error in his thinking, wanted to shake the priest's hand, and ask for forgiveness. Meeting in person was a profound—and rare—moment of grace in a horrific conflict.

Religion aims to provide answers, but it's also dishonest. Religion can be the incense and effigy and ancient robes of a region's conflict, but these disguise the root of the conflict: politics. For many disenfranchised, standing up for a time-honored belief system is far more honorable than supporting the personal agendas of flawed men.

Northern Ireland was the perfect example of this dynamic.

Embracing moments that tune us into our state of being—as Harry did on the chairlift, as I did beside a lily pond in England, as Father Troy did when he shook hands with someone who once thought to kill him—is the closest we'll come to our inner selves that may or may not live on after that final waystation.

Though I cheated death in the mountains many times, I never believed that I robbed some afterlife of the natural order of things. Instead, I became a captive audience to each vulnerable moment, focused on the white smoke of my exhales lifting at elevation, and appreciated that I was still around to hear the occasional low hum of life's gears. These moments of grace moved me past my ugliness in life.

People change.

For years, I celebrated the spring equinox by driving to Saint Mary's Glacier, sliding a pair of skis inside a backpack, hiking up a large snow field above the lake, then skiing down the remnant glacier. Because the jaunt was fairly close, in Idaho Springs, the ritual was an easy way to celebrate the upcoming hiking season and get my legs in shape.

On that spring day of 2000, I arrived at the parking area to discover no other cars around.

Excellent. Solitude and a ton of snow.

I laced up my boots, secured my skis, and began a deliberate pace for the quarter mile to the lake. Terrain surrounding the lake was nearly impossible with powder. I rounded the lake's far end and began a stair-step, toe-kicking climb up the snow field.

Increasingly, the wind became problematic.

When I reached the plateau above the lake, I had to crouch so gusts wouldn't blow me off the mountain. Two hours of effort had gotten me only as far as the spot where the snow usually ended in spring. This time, the snow field stretched as far as I could see.

My target was James Peak, a thirteen-thousand-foot mountain with a broad southern slope to climb up and a radically steep east face to swish down. Another half mile, and I was there.

Breathing hard, legs tired, I switched into ski boots and hiked up another hundred feet to gain some downhill speed. I snapped into my bindings, paused momentarily to look out at the sameness of the snow-covered terrain, and let out a cry of triumph.

All mine to enjoy.

I jumped into my first turn, then nailed my second and third. Soon, I reached the flat terrain I crossed earlier. My momentum slowed, so it was time to use my poles to leverage the conditions. I lifted my arms. The nemesis of my earlier challenge—the wind—pushed me across the open landscape like I wore a wingsuit. I laughed as if the lazy perk were a reward for the exhausting effort to summit.

I coasted right across the slope, reasoning that the alternate route around the lake put me closer to the trees and the road, thus eliminating a long hike to the car to haul my gear. It was efficient, just the way I liked my outdoors. The wind carried me fast.

Then faster.

And faster still.

The support beneath my edges *sounded* different.

No longer fine powder. No longer silent.

Crustier.

Oh god. My speed and the right-lake route made it impossible to turn back. Bearing on my downhill edges and maintaining a solid relationship with the snowpack were the only things keeping me from sliding into the lake and drowning. The gray-white landscape blended with the overcast sky.

Ground became air; air became ground.

At any moment, I'd be underwater, unable to surface because my feet were strapped to skis like a boat anchor. The water's temperature would be a thousand simultaneous ice axes.

The precise sound of my skis cutting through ice and gravitational forces acting against my body were my only true indicators that time and my body moved forward, that I still had a chance, and that the yawning white monster of hubris had not swallowed me.

Left to my own devices, things might have ended there. The wind—the perilous, noble wind—scurried me across the slope above the lake surface and saved me.

At the trees, I popped out of my skis and collapsed. My knees were gelatin. I sucked in greedy lungfuls of air and reasoned my way back out of panic. My decision to go right—to defy the route I knew to be safe for years of prior spring equinoxes to save hiking steps to the car—had nearly cost me my life. I reasoned that was the way it was in the high country. The next innocuous decision always had the potential to become the last decision.

When I returned home, Darlene glanced up from her book and asked, "Did you have fun?"

I managed a smile and nodded. She could not know how the yellow warmth of light over her shoulder, how her innocent question, hit me that evening. She could never know, but I knew.

The remaining peaks would only get more treacherous. She was a gift. My girls were a gift.

And I was a fool who couldn't stop.

In mid-August, I decided to make another attempt to summit Mount Tabeguache and Mount Shavano. This time, I packed more common sense. I asked the mountain to be kind and allow me safe passage. The hike went perfectly. I summited both peaks in one day without incident and returned safely. I found this approach to settle better around my bones—coming at the Fourteeners from a place of respect, not as simply a conquest and a checkmark on a list. I looked forward to reaching my half goal before summer ended.

Mount of the Holy Cross was a leg burner: twelve hiking miles and an elevation gain of more than five thousand six hundred feet. The day was spectacular. I ascended a ridge that brought Holy Cross into view, then descended almost a thousand feet to East Cross Creek so that I might reach switchbacks to the opposite ridge. The final section was a challenging six hundred vertical feet of talus slope to the summit.

Holy Cross, the northernmost mountain of the Sawatch mountain range, with its Bowl of Tears Lake and cross-patterned couloir below the summit, was the bookend of a line of fifteen mountains over fourteen thousand feet. I had accomplished both summits of this range in the same summer by reaching the Angel of Shavano one week earlier. Two weeks later, Huron Peak proved easy and prepared me for the next, much harder climb.

Pyramid Peak, from Maroon Lake, looks like a pyramid. In three short miles, the ascent requires hiking over four thousand four hundred feet in three stages. The first mile, from the Maroon Lake Trailhead, is a series of switchbacks rising from ten thousand feet to nearly twelve thousand feet. My lungs reached for air as I tried to maintain a steady pace. A few times I stopped to catch my breath.

At the top of the switchbacks, I looked out over a large basin of snow and boulder-sized ice chunks to the mountain's base. I craned my neck and took in a most imposing mountain. Ahead of me was a small group of climbers starting up the left side of the ridge above the basin—the route recommended in guidebooks as the easiest to the summit.

Easiest rarely held my interest, and following a group threatened the peace I chased on every peak. I veered right and climbed what appeared to be a similar ascent.

It wasn't.

The seven-hundred-foot ascent on the northwest ridge went as planned until I reached the mountain's real pyramid. I could not find a clear route up.

Eventually I settled upon an upward angle around the middle of the mountain that required scrambling above steep gullies. At this point I was nearly three-quarters of the way around the mountain. At a group of rock ledges, I looked for a path that might take me higher, yet saw no cairns marking a route. I had climbed into a predicament: reach the ledges above, not knowing if they lead to the summit, or find myself stranded with no way down. To get higher required leaps upward to grasp the rock ledge and pull myself up. Without a safety net. Without ropes. A leap of free-climbing faith.

The view below bottomed out my stomach. Miscalculation would lead to certain death. Reluctantly, I retraced my route back to the basin and followed the leftward direction the other climbers had taken. I lost hours, but I was alive. I considered it a win.

Reaching the summit in the late afternoon was not what I planned. My descent would have to be quicker to return to the car before dark. Hurried timeframes led to carelessness, but I allowed myself a few moments to take photos. One of the pictures captured a rather unremarkable crevice at eye level on South Maroon Peak.

The following summer, the crevice was not so unremarkable.

Castle Peak 14,265' | Conundrum 14,022' | South Maroon 14,156' | Handies 14,048' | Capitol Peak 14,130'

Chapter Seven

In early July, I struck out for the highest summit in the Elk Mountain Range: Castle Peak. Castle has a boring, monotonous approach with bleak-looking switchbacks that seem unnecessarily long. Loose scree makes foot placement uncertain. A few hours past the trailhead, I spotted one of the hike's most redeeming features: the Montezuma silver mine remnants. I contemplated how miners could have survived conditions at thirteen thousand feet during the winter. Besides sleep, after working a mine until exhaustion, how did miners occupy their remaining hours while buried in snow and ice for months? Likely, quite a bit of alcohol, both to warm the blood and pass the time.

Technically, nearby Conundrum Peak has enough summit elevation at 14,040 feet to be considered a Fourteener, but it lacks the elevation-loss criteria between peaks. To be listed as an official Fourteener in Colorado, a mountain must gain and lose three hundred feet of prominence to be considered a separate peak. Thanks to an early start and good weather, I summited Castle, then scooped up an achievement on Conundrum, a short ridge away. Castle brought me to thirty-one peaks, twenty of them solo.

Fourteen peaks remained, but at forty-eight years old, recovery took several days. Some level of pain over the summer climbing season was now a near-constant companion. I felt the ticking of life's clock as surely as the contractions of my atria and ventricles on an ambitious slope. I worried that I wouldn't complete the rest before my body gave out. I resolved to tackle a few hard peaks, sooner rather than later.

Shortly after the children returned to Northern Ireland in late August, I traveled to Aspen, the billionaire's playground, to attempt a solo climb of South Maroon. In stark contrast to the area's typical private jet and Gucci lifestyle, my routine was a good start to the next day's climb by sleeping in the back of my eyesore wagon. I parked at the lot closest to the trailhead and stretched out in the back with a blanket. In the fading twilight, I glanced up at the dark monolith of the Maroon Bells, two of the state's steepest and most dangerous peaks.

I had to be nuts to do South Maroon solo.

A blinking light near the base of North Maroon caught my eye. I squinted and watched it repeat as the minutes stretched long. It was clearly a sign of distress. Sadly, the night ahead was long, and rescue would not arrive until morning.

At sunrise, the rescue team gathered around my wagon like

locusts—quick, with a powerful presence. I stumbled out of the car and learned that a climber had fallen on North Maroon and broken his leg. The distress light. I imagined his night: a lot of pain, most likely no tent, and a few people staying with him to keep him as comfortable as possible. I reflected on my North Maroon summit three years earlier: the two attempts, the glazed rock when the snow arrived, the climber above yelling, 'Rocks!' as Vince and I made eye contact. One of the peak's greatest dangers was dislodging your footing onto other climbers or losing it out from under you. When any mountaineer hears of such things, it's natural for fear to seep through the crevices. The ability to push past those slimy and traitorous hitches of self-preservation in the stomach is the degree to which the climber has built confidence on the lesser peaks.

And, probably, the degree to which the climber is a little nuts.

Dawn came cool and clear. Passing Maroon Lake on my left, just as the morning light spilled into the valley, I spotted a large bundle of sticks in the water's middle and a beaver swimming to its lodge. Everything was calm.

Uncomfortably calm.

Menacingly calm.

I knew not to let down my guard.

Pyramid Peak rose steeply and strongly to the left. I saluted it, grateful I had made its summit the prior year. I continued to seek the trail's turnoff to South Maroon and wondered if I had missed it. The beginning of an idyllic hike gradually shifted to one of concern. I was well past the mountain I planned to ascend. Should I retrace my route or keep going?

Every Fourteener has that moment—a full sixty-second pause of *what now?* followed by indecision that stops forward progress. Climbing is nothing if not five hundred micro-decisions on the way to glory. Knowing that one out of the five hundred might kill requires a seasoned watchfulness.

And then, a push past it.

Screw it.

I bushwhacked up the slope, determined to find a unique path. The steepness surprised me. At times, I slipped and clung to small bushes to keep from sliding downhill. Gradually, the terrain became all rock and almost vertical. A cleft in the mountain face above looked like a path to the ridge and then the summit. I scrambled higher to a cut where the sides were three or four feet apart but straight up and faced a choice: slide down the slope and give up the day or free climb higher and hope I wasn't cliffing out.

Ability versus safety.

Ultimately, confidence edged out fear.

The next moments would be the most critical and dangerous I faced on my quest.

Wind silenced. Birds crazy enough to be at that elevation hushed. I intentionally decentered inhales and exhales from my awareness—not a spare ounce of focus on anything but the open air below me and the next foothold and handhold. And the next. And the next. No thoughts of family, work, life. No thoughts of Daniel or Vince or of falling. Nothing but a solid four-point placement before testing my weight against what came next. The narrow figment of survival threaded through the lens of every. next. choice.

So close to dying, I had never felt so alive.

Forty additional climbing feet brought me to the top of the cleft. In less than an hour, I summited South Maroon. My heart was a windsock, pliable and at the mercy of every gale that had come my way but capable of soaring had it not been tethered to my screaming limbs.

I had conquered one of Colorado's most dangerous peaks alone.

Standing on the summit, looking out over North Maroon and

Pyramid—demanding peaks I had conquered—I replayed my ascent sequence on South Maroon and, rather foolishly, allowed the danger to slip beneath the surface. I still had to descend, by far the more difficult of the two halves of any mountain. That fear ushered good, healthy common sense back in. Since I hadn't found the regular trail on the way up, I couldn't go back the same route. I retraced the ridge, passed by the cleft I had climbed, and decided on a route that appeared safer.

Safer did not equate to easier.

By the time I reached Maroon Creek and pulled off my right boot and sock, my big toe had bled out beneath the nail. Pain from the constant downward pressure seemed a fair bargain for staying otherwise unharmed as if the universe were a weighing scale and I'd heaped too much on the plate that held all the mercy. I glanced up at where I'd been.

The visual path stole my breath.

Did I do that?

Man wasn't designed for such impossibilities.

And yet...

In theory, on paper, and in every conceivable way, I have used up my lives.

Around this point in my quest, my outlook switched from time logged on the trails of the easier Fourteeners to serious contemplation of the risk ahead. I have never put into words the mental gymnastics required to surmount possible death by choice. But I endangered myself for this tangible goal; at the very least, I owe it to those I love and those who might be considering such a feat to be honest.

In the days and weeks ahead of a Fourteener, I choked up on my mental game. The remaining peaks required more effort, planning, and, often, an elongated commitment of time and driving distance. They also carried greater expectations and demanded extra everything. I did not confess my worries to Darlene. Had I told her of the self-flagellation and pain that awaited me, the increased potential of making her a widow, and that some other man down the road, a safe man who didn't push his luck, might someday be the one to walk my daughters down the aisle, and that possibility was a near constant source of heartbreak, she might have reasoned me free of all fifty-five peaks.

She would have been right; she was always right.

Instead, I would walk out the door, thinking, *Tonight, if I don't make it back, it's okay.* The hesitation wasn't there.

And that makes me the most selfish sonofabitch in the lives of those I love.

Maybe it is the gradual desensitizing that comes from accomplishing lesser peaks. Likely, something is missing in me, in mountaineers and adventure-seekers, that protects us from ourselves. When most hear something like the unfortunate account of a young man in the high country, fully geared and helmeted, who thought he could point his snowboard straight downhill, launch himself off an incline, and clear an entire two-lane road, there is judgment: *what was he thinking? Does he have a death wish?* My brain goes to different questions: *did he not have enough speed? How does an accomplished snowboarder make such a miscalculation? What factors did he fail to account for?* It is a judgment-free zone between my head and my heart. But for the grace of something beyond me, a dozen miscalculations might have led to my end as well.

Thirty years past the start of my quest, I suspect younger mountaineers now chase different things toward the same end.

Look past the GoPro on the helmet. Look beyond the near-instant gratification of follower comments on a live stream at ten thousand feet elevation. Look beneath the slick and well-coordinated wool and synthetic fibers of an endorsement deal. I am not so cynical as to believe that those who chase mountains behind me are superficial.

On the trail, I pass plenty of younger kindred spirits. On occasion, we exchange words. They, too, love the outdoors. They desire experiences that transcend the visual-heavy world of video games and hi-def cinematic drone shots to a subcutaneous understanding that embraces the kinesthetic. In an augmented medium, we all experience the same inputs. But in nature?

Boundless inputs.

Boundless realities.

Inside the nature of things also lies spirituality; inside our society is a latent hunger for meaning that is increasingly absent in organized faith. And beyond that spirituality is a sort of enchanted component to it all. When finger placement equals life, when a high-focus functionality is required to sustain you bodily, mentally, and emotionally, the self is tapping on the door of a consciousness that can only be described as mystical.

And who wouldn't be spellbound by that possibility?

What are we thinking?

We aren't. We *feel.*

Do we have a death wish?

Equal to that of a life wish.

And if we don't make it back?

It's okay. We are okay. We're just boundless sonofabitches.

I crossed Handies Peak off my list on Labor Day weekend. At three miles and an elevation gain of only 2500 feet from the American basin angle, Handies is a short and relatively featureless climb, apart from the eagle's eye view of Sloan Lake. The vista of the San Juan Mountain range from the clouds is stunning. I made this thirty-third summit alongside Wayne. Glissading down a massive snow field to mark summer's end is peak amusement, though I did bruise my tailbone on a hidden rock. After the innocuousness of such a mild peak, I needed to tackle something more substantial.

Friends who crave the Fourteener experience—even just one for accomplishment's sake—often asked if they could join me on the next peak. I don't always know their physicality and endurance, how much time they've spent conditioning, or how their bodies will react at altitude. But I always believed that everyone has agency over their journey and choices and that there is value in hiking the trails without always summiting. Such was the case with Ken. I had slated the weekend after Handies to climb Capitol, where Daniel had died. That day dawned with a dull ache behind my breastbone, a slurry of memories, and the pallor of seriousness to the climb. Having someone less experienced with me added sharpness to it all, so I made sure we had the tough conversation before we set out: *I'm going to the top. You should go as far as you're comfortable.*

We had camped at Capitol Lake the previous night to get a jump start at eleven thousand feet. Day two started with a steep ascent to the saddle of Mount Daly, a thirteen-thousand-foot peak connecting Capitol to a sub-summit known as K-2. Daly has a steep dimple on one side and vertical rock faces on the other. At the saddle, our hike took us off-trail to the mountain's backside. I puzzled out a route up and began testing the viability of some rock ledges. That's when Ken spoke up.

"Anthony, this is starting to make me uncomfortable. I think this is as far as I can go. Why don't I head back and wait for you?"

Pressure in my chest eased. I had worried about Ken more than I realized. "That's probably best. It's getting tricky."

We parted ways with plans to meet where the ridge dropped back to the trail. I found my way up and around the rock faces to reach the Knife Edge. Guidebooks had detailed this stretch of Capitol as an intimidating section where the mountain falls away close to a thousand feet on both sides. The usual recommendation is to get across by straddling the solid rock and scooting its twenty-foot length. Once through, the ascent to the summit was described as easier.

In person, the stretch was a Class four axe blade with zero margin for error.

I didn't feel comfortable straddling the rock. Instead, I side-walked, utilizing cracks in the granite for feet and fingers. As tempting as it is to judge others for humping the Knife Edge to make it across, the perspective on the blade is the stuff of frozen fear. Lowering the center of gravity makes sense. Climbers give each other the time and space to avoid becoming the peak's next casualty.

The summit was spectacular—ruggedly majestic and hard-won. Capitol had been as much of an emotional battle as a physical one. While I rested my body, memories of Daniel visited. I dedicated the hike to him and wished for his wife and children that their new path without him would be peaceful.

Knowing Ken waited for me, I did not remain at the top for long. Recrossing the Knife Edge in the same manner brought a tremendous sense of relief. Despite the serious downclimb awaiting me, I was on the usual route and high-spirited from realizing I had only sixteen peaks left in my quest.

To save time going up and over the sub-summit of K-2, I cut across a forty-degree indent of the mountain that connected with the ridge. The concave section of the slope was spongy and unstable—nothing at all like the Knife Edge stone. Halfway across, fully committed in either direction, I realized I was in trouble. Any slip of the hands or feet would be disastrous. My tactic shifted to a crab walk—painstakingly guarded, ginger in movement while I tested each placement before shifting my weight, face planted into the mountainside. Time slowed.

When I reached the far edge of the indent, I did something I don't often do while climbing: I looked back and down. I studied how far I might have tumbled had I lost my footing. Most summit days, nothing good comes from such a dalliance of the mind. It's a cheap adrenaline rush to entertain what might have gone wrong but didn't, and it lowers defenses and focus best used for what remains ahead.

I reunited with Ken. Though I was relieved to see him, that our plan had come to fruition and he had enjoyed a day on Capitol, the chasm between our experiences was oceanic. My gut was a tumble of knife blades and poor decisions to save time and mourning someone who had died while I made it out. The abyss of quietness lasted all day, through the hike down to our camp, through packing our gear and trekking out, until I reached home and called Daniel's climbing friend, Mike.

The Knife Edge or the forty-degree-Jello slope? I had to know where Daniel had fallen.

"He was always so careful," Mike said.

I hadn't known that about Daniel. We had only ever climbed Yale together.

Mike recounted Daniel's route. He fell at the same stretch where I had crab-walked.

"A hundred-and-fifty-foot fall. Died instantly." Silence on the line lengthened until Mike added, "His last word was 'Rocks!'" A practice of all climbers to take ownership of loosening the slope.

Daniel's final act when the mountain gave way was to protect others.

Summer evenings in Colorado's mountain towns are eclectic and surreal. Louisville's Town Square is no exception. Storefronts spill outward with artisanal gifts and clusters of colorful blooms. Delicious street-fare aromas waft through the crisp air to the 360-degree, picturesque backdrop. Acoustic musicians dot the strolling lanes and gather clusters of passersby who gravitate to the natural vibe in the unpolished, perfect theater.

It was here that a stranger tapped me on the shoulder.

"Have you done them all?" she asked.

All? My mind raced with what she meant.

She smiled and pointed to the back of my t-shirt.

I glanced down, remembering what shirt I had absently pulled on that morning: a well-worn, semi-faded one with all of Colorado's Fourteeners listed on the back. Her question suddenly made sense.

"I have," I said over the band's noise.

She nodded. "Me too."

We compared our respective quests, trading stories and timelines. About ten minutes into our exchange, I said, "It wasn't all good times. Some of my hiking companions died on the mountains."

She pressed her lips together, all but erasing her easy smile. This time, her "Me too" held a somber timbre.

"It took me a while to get past Daniel."

"Daniel?"

"Daniel Leaman."

She pressed her fingers to her lips, to hold back words, breath, something. Tears pooled. "I was six feet from him when he fell."

My heart felt as if it had been lobbed off a ten-thousand-foot rim shelf.

The music ended. Passersby clapped absently then moved on about their evenings as if the most remarkable thing had not happened, as if they had all the time in this life to eat roasted Olathe corn cobs, buy red chokecherry jam, and smell the sweet alyssum, while Daniel had not.

We found a pair of seats. She was a traveler of sorts, meant to find me to bring me the story. I cannot say that it would have changed my choices if I had met her sooner, before all the peaks were behind me, but I gathered myself again into deliberate exhales and recognized the moment for what it was: a gift. She had stayed with Daniel's body on Capitol for three days through adverse weather while authorities worked to retrieve him from the mountain.

No climber left behind.

She was another reminder from the universe of how lucky I had been. My risks should have killed me, but I was still here.

What started as a desire to be in a select company, to do something memorable to justify the time and effort required, to check summit names off a list before I reached the peak of my physicality and it was all downhill from there, had shifted to a transcendent microcosm of the human experience: pain and pleasure, failure and achievement, hubris and humility. Gain and loss. I began the quest because I am ordinary. Forgettable in every way, in all stages of life, but that's not quite how it ended.

I was still here. I vowed to make the most of it.

Summers in Colorado are eclectic and surreal. That seventh year of my quest was no exception. I gravitated to the unpolished, perfect theater of the Elk Range. I contemplated last words and final acts. And inside a 360-degree, picturesque backdrop, I settled into a single-mindedness to keep pushing ahead.

If I don't make it back, it's okay.

Capitol had allowed me to live. That day was September 9, 2001.

Two days later, I was to fly to New York.

*Uncompahgre Peak 14,309' | Mount Wilson 14,246' |
Wetterhorn Peak 14,015' | Humboldt 14,064' | Crestone East 14,294' | Mount Sneffels
14,150' | Crestone Needle 14,197' |
Kit Carson 14,165' | San Luis 14,014'*

Chapter Eight

Eight to eleven years into the quest

My younger brother, Curtis, pushed limits in other ways.

Body-shattering ways. Heroic ways.

As a teenage motocross rider, he broke his leg when another rider kicked over his bike on a turn. In his twenties, he drove a local camper's ATV off a mountain at night, which resulted in him being placed in a halo with four screws in his skull. He spent six months healing fractures in his back, neck, leg, and ribs. And on that autumn day in 2001, when terrorists flew planes into the Twin Towers of Manhattan,

Curtis brought every bit of his years as a firefighter and his self-made high-rise disaster expertise to Ground Zero.

He talked his way past the police roadblocks and tunnel checkpoints. For the next ten days, he assisted with the immediate search and recovery process of nearby but badly damaged buildings. In the evenings, he helped the FBI and FEMA determine the nature of the toxic materials in the smoldering ruins and advised the emergency incident command team of their findings. Though he had access to air quality data, it didn't take a genius to realize that the cloud hanging over the area and the incessant coughing of all those present was a toxic recipe for serious health issues down the road. Still, those in charge wanted to craft a narrative that averted panic and mass flight from the area. Incensed by the official statements regarding Ground Zero air quality safety for first responders, Curtis did everything he could to elevate awareness for his comrades.

I never made it to the airport on September 11, 2001. After receiving a call from someone at my company headquarters to turn on the television, I tried to phone Curtis. In our business life, we often tried to coordinate cities in which to reconnect. That week, it was to be New York City. His office relayed that his plane had made it as far as Washington, D.C., before all flights were grounded and that he had paid a cab driver an exorbitant amount of money to drive him into Manhattan.

That was the last they'd heard from him.

As the youngest of the four brothers, Curtis was more removed from the stark recollections of abuse cemented in late childhood. Though we don't often venture into specifics out of self-preservation, I know he remembers Dad pounding Doug into a kitchen wall so hard that the drywall dented. I know he recalls us climbing atop Dad on several occasions to stop him from beating Mom because Curtis was there beside me, blocking the violence. Still, I believed he set the incidents aside, perhaps not trusting their viability against the unreliability of memories at such a young age. Long after the older of us had distanced ourselves from a toxic father and a mother who refused to hold him accountable, Curtis remained.

The year of the McCain-Obama presidential election changed all that. Curtis was out of the country on business. Though he had yet to decide for whom he wanted to cast his vote, he entrusted Dad to fill out his absentee ballot and mail it in. "I'll let you know when I decide," Curtis told him. A week or so later, he asked Dad to fill out his ballot for Obama. In a very stilted, formal language via email, Dad agreed to honor his wishes. Upon arrival back in the States, with Dad at the airport, Curtis mentioned the election.

"Did you turn in my ballot?"

Dad shook his head. "I couldn't let you vote for that black bastard."

The unapologetically racist statement was an explosive backdraft in the already oxygen-depleted environment of their relationship. On the way home, the argument turned vitriolic. Dad refused to believe he had raised a son who would vote for a black man. Curtis demanded an apology that never came. The moment Dad balled up his fists, Curtis walked out the door and out of their lives. True to his word, he never communicated with Dad again.

In the ensuing years, Mom tried unsuccessfully to bring everyone together, to make amends for wrongs that were not hers. Curtis and I were different—a subset of hope in the ruins of a nuclear family. I took his call then and each time after. We grew close. I enjoyed his company immensely. Camping in nature healed us, as individuals and together. Around the campfires, we discussed life and reconnected as brothers. The mountains became our psychological couch.

It wasn't all highbrow growth. If either of us complained of being tired, the other would respond with, "You're such a wimp." Leaving a quiet cloud of gas in the air for the other to discover usually generated the response, "You bastard." And always, after a good day of hiking, gathering wood, setting up camp, and reclining in our chairs with the fire roaring, we clinked wine glasses and said, "Up yours."

We shared many memorable times. On Independence Day one year, we were snowed out on Rabbit Ears Pass near Steamboat Springs. On the same camping trip where I accidentally drove my wagon down a ski slope, swarms of mosquitos drove us from our camp near Monarch Pass. Camping at the ten-thousand-foot Flat Tops Wilderness was incredible until the rumble of evening storms hit so close that it vibrated the rib cage.

Whether traversing high mountain plateaus, looking across colossal and stratified canyons, or discovering cliff-face caves that went so deep into the mountainside that only headlamps would uncover its secrets, being in nature with Curtis became my greatest joy. We'd walk clearings late at night, gaze up at the Milky Way, and ponder skies so clear that the cloud clusters were believable galaxies. We toasted shooting stars and leaned into the companionable and safe silence of best friends.

Eventually, I wanted to share my Fourteener journey with him. After his mini, lower-altitude accomplishments of Grizzly Creek, Deep Creek Canyons, and the Weminuche Wilderness built his confidence, he wanted to hike Wetterhorn Peak in honor of his many friends and fellow firefighters who had died in the 9/11 collapse of the Twin Towers.

Wetterhorn is astonishingly beautiful. Grassy basins and boulder fields that have the potential to categorize this hike as a long and boring slog give way to exciting exposures and class-three scrambles. Its named wall is intimidating until a close-up study reveals ladder-like ledges that allow for a good, solid climb. The summit offers picturesque views of foliage in the valley and incredible vistas of nearby Matterhorn and Uncompahgre and beyond.

Curtis raised a hand of victory at the top. Stamina driven by grief is a powerful reservoir for achievement. When words came through his labored exhales, his voice tightened around them. So, too, did mine. His ribs were mine. It was 2003. Losses were still raw.

That summer, hosting children from Northern Ireland was the calmest we could remember. There were no mass shootings or bombings, and all our kids and host families had a wonderful time. The peaceful pause renewed my desire to tackle my final list of peaks.

Three of them presented as difficult a challenge as any I had faced: the Wilson Group. El Diente, Wilson Peak, and Mount Wilson are some of the most rugged peaks in the state. To reach this isolated area of southwestern Colorado, near the picturesque ski town of Telluride, required a seven-hour drive to the trailhead. The San Juan Mountain range is as beautiful as any part of the country, but it hides darkness and dangers for ill-equipped mountaineers.

Rejoining my hiking partner, Wayne, whom I had met on Mount Lindsey four years earlier, our first day began by attempting the summit of Wilson Peak. From the Navajo Basin trailhead, the ascent of fifty-three hundred feet in less than five miles was arduous, requiring regular collaboration on how to traverse a series of cliffs before climbing the last one thousand feet over a series of undulating broken rocks to reach the top. We continuously asked each other questions—"What do you think?" and "How does it look to you?"—then followed them with responses like, "Let me climb up a little and take a look." This collaborative method helped us successfully reach the summit. Wayne and I were stoked. The terrain offered valuable intel on what Mount Wilson and El Diente held for us.

The next day, following the same trail into the Navajo Basin at twelve thousand feet, we turned to what we thought was Mount Wilson, only to discover after reaching the summit that we had accidentally climbed a thirteen thousand nine-hundred-foot mountain called Gladstone Peak. Located between Wilson Peak and Mount Wilson, we could only look off to the west in disappointment. From thousands of feet below, it had been difficult to determine if we were climbing the correct trail. We took solace that at least we were on top of a mountain, seeing what we were made of. Reluctantly, we began our descent, knowing we had reached only one of the Fourteeners, but we agreed to return the following year for the remaining two. It was early August so there was still time for me to knock out a few more solos—Humboldt and East Crestone.

With Wayne as my willing partner the next July and August, we tackled Mount Sneffles, Crestone Needle, and Kit Carson Peak.

Crestone Needle brought us into the company of a French couple who pitched a tent that hung suspended off the two-thousand-foot vertical face of Ellingwood Arete. The elite climbers, well beyond my skill class, with the entire Alps as a backyard playground, sought the best of what Colorado had to offer.

On day two of our Sangre de Cristo jaunt, Wayne and I left our camp at the Spanish Creek trailhead, headed for Challenger Point Peak, a 14,087-foot subpeak on the northwest shoulder of the parent summit of Kit Carson. So named in memory of the astronauts who lost their lives in the Challenger explosion, a small plaque on the summit reads: *Challenger Point, 14080+', In Memory of the Crew of Shuttle Challenger, Seven who died accepting the risk, expanding Mankind's horizons, January 28, 1986.* The Latin phrase *Ad Astra Per Aspera,* which translates as *to the stars through adversity,* finishes the dedication.

Wayne's familiarity with the area made the hike easier, but after Challenger Point, his demeanor shifted. He returned to our campsite instead of continuing to Kit Carson's summit. On a solo ascent of Kit Carson, Wayne had lost his footing a few years earlier and tumbled face-first on a descent through a scree field. A broken nose and a busted-up face certainly accounted for his reticence to redo the peak. We parted ways, and I went on to the connecting saddle, successfully crossing Kit Carson off my list.

At the top, a thunderstorm quickly developed and left me hyper-exposed to the elements. I climbed down into a rock-filled gully with chimney sidewalls to avoid the lightning and wait for improved conditions. After an hour, the storm subsided. I continued my descent, but I could only guess the proper direction without Wayne's expertise on the mountain. The gully rocks were shifty, exactly as Wayne had described in his tumble, so I balanced the necessity for a thoughtful and careful route with the cold and dark pressing me to move faster. Never had I been so grateful to see a campfire. Wayne had prepared a robust blaze so I could find my way and warm immediately.

Years of climbs ran together. The many details, once so vivid, began to fade into sketchy recollections unless a peak had some kind of *event* attributed to it—*event* usually attributed to misfortune or adversity. I was at forty peaks. My body was aging. I had to press on.

⁂

"Bro, we're going to make a great team," Curtis said. "Kick butt and take names with the business. Have more time to hang together—hiking and camping. You won't miss your old job."

My brother offered me a way out—a way to resign and come work for him that released me from the stress and oppression of trying to fit into an upper-management corporate dynamic that had shifted and subverted at every turn. Curtis' business was a fit for me on several levels. We were closer than ever and of a like mind and work ethic. He appreciated what I brought to the table. I looked forward to bringing my management skills to the successful high-rise disaster response consulting business that Curtis had built.

But our worlds could not have been more different.

He came to his client's problems from a symbiotic background. As a former firefighter, Curtis's credibility was next-level and inspired. While I struggled to find common talking points with new customers, Curtis regaled them with life-and-death stories from his experience that underscored the importance of his services. Regurgitating what Curtis said was neither authentic nor successful. The new business I brought in wasn't enough to cover expenses.

Self-doubt gave way to self-criticism. Once again, I was unimpactful and utterly forgettable in every way. What had I been thinking? I'd left my career path, nearly burning a bridge by foolishly declaring to senior management that I felt *free at last*, traded stress for anxious feelings of imposter syndrome, and possibly compromised a business Curtis had worked so hard to establish.

I returned home from the high of a Fourteener accomplishment to a phone call from Curtis.

"I can't carry you any longer. I don't have the cash flow to give you more time to figure this out. I'm sorry, Anthony."

He was gentle with it all. No amount of business or income was worth trading how far we had come as brothers and friends. Still, I struggled with the dissonance between the fantasy of new horizons and the reality that I wasn't good enough. I told him I understood. I did. That didn't make the conversation any easier.

"At least I got one deal for you in Los Angeles. That should cover some of my expenses," I said. "I have a few more irons in the fire. I'll get them over to you."

We didn't talk again for many months. Our interactions would have been a trash stew of awkwardness, familial adversity, and failed expectations—something neither of us wanted to revisit after the childhood we'd endured. I was a middle-aged man, cliffed out on a formidable mountain of looming unemployment, with only a few months of cash in the bank and a wife and two little girls to support. How had I miscalculated so badly? Would my girls be ashamed of me?

Depression set in. Latent memories of my father struggling to put food on the table for a family of six surfaced. As an enlisted man, being home meant lower pay and more parenting stress. Deployment equated to more pay for hazard duty and allowed sailors to blow off steam with drinking and fighting. I was keenly aware of the predisposition in my ancestry to turn to the bottle. Old cycles of familiarity breathed down my neck. I had to find a way out.

In desperation, I humbly inquired if my former employer would be interested in having me back. Reaching out to a few contacts, I found the response promising. Frankly, I would have accepted any offer. After what seemed like an interminable length of time, word came that there was a place for me, and it wouldn't require relocation. Though I wouldn't be able to start until October, relief swept through me.

Mom was born and raised in Dublin. Remnants of four hundred years of British occupation were still a festering wound in her family's collective memory. Her father abused alcohol, and her mother cautioned her on several occasions against marrying an Irishman. Problems were far more complex than mere genetics. Generational traumas of famines and economic downturns related to British subjugation made it difficult for the Irish who chose not to emigrate elsewhere to secure jobs and pull themselves out of poverty. Local boys provided little escape from her home situation beyond trading one set of problems for another family's secrets. Dad was a nice-looking, clean-cut military man from America who wrote love letters that included original poems that put Longfellow to shame and injected straight into her veins.

She ignored that he did the same for many other girls.

Hers was a choice born of fairy tales—strategic, economically driven, a foreign prince with Hollywood features and a poet's tongue. There were few early signs of plot twists to come.

For his part, she was beautiful and kind. Certainly, a fairy tale. He had his choice of woman, but at nineteen, she was chosen.

Her mother went to London to meet him, this pen pal who had written prolifically to her daughter for two years. Family lore has it that he checked out, all on the up and up, and that they smoked cigarettes and got drunk together.

No doubt, she saw Warren Massey as an improvement for her daughter beyond the prospects she had.

When the economy had collapsed with the Depression, her father, James Heatley, went from being a dapper man about town with a nice house who rode a horse and sported a monocle to losing his import business and drinking up his family's food money, leaving them desperately hungry. To add further indignity to my grandfather's legacy, he swindled my father out of the money for his daughter's engagement ring. As it turned out, James's *import business* was likely a front for his double life as a paymaster—someone who delivered funds—for the Irish Republican Army, the IRA. He drove a lemon drop truck, a front of candy sales and delivery that secreted weapons across the country. At British checkpoints, soldiers asked him what was in the back of his truck. He'd joke about candy—what else?—give the soldiers a bit of sweets, and no one was the wiser.

There is no official record of James Heatley serving with the IRA, but I have the Polaroids of his casket draped with the Irish flag and soldiers firing volleys of rounds over his grave, an indication of a full IRA burial honors.

Regardless of the specifics of my grandfather's double life, our Irish lineage is messy with secrets, violence, working-class blues, and more than a little taste for alcohol. They scraped by with limited resources, felt the painful echoes of the potato famine only two generations removed, and harbored deep resentment toward the British, who made the famine worse by insisting on the export of what little food supply existed in Ireland to meet market quota. This trauma proved a motivating part of the collective Irish identity—stubborn, proud, and obsessively focused on stockpiling food.

The echoes of this carried all the way to our family in Virginia.

When James died at the age of seventy, my grandmother already showed signs of cognitive impairment. Relatives in London didn't know what to do with her, so we accepted her into our home. A volatile marriage and four energetic teenage boys made for a dramatic mix.

Grandma Heatley wasn't a storyteller. She sat in her chair, read, chain-smoked cigarettes, and fixed family meals. In my mind, she occupied space but did not engage. Smart woman. Only once did she try to break up a fight between Doug and me. She ended up with a broken thumb and effectively learned her lesson that we were all a lost cause. So, when my father slipped into drunken episodes and the violence came, there was nothing to be done but listen or remove herself from the space. Gone were the days of her advice to my mother: *don't marry an Irishman*. My father hadn't ended on the up and up, either. Men had proven a consistent disappointment. When she became forgetful enough to leave burning pots on the stove and roamed clear of the garden, my parents put her in a memory care facility until she passed.

Her story was not unique. It isn't hard to understand the desperation that led to political uprisings against British oppression. It's a complex relationship—the Irish and the British—made all the more compelling by the turning tide in Irish sentiment around the time of independence in 1922. Subsequent generations aimed to leave the refuse in the past. A large portion of the hatred faded away. After an eight-hundred-year struggle, Ireland finally had what it had always coveted. It didn't mean the wrongs were forgotten—Irish sentiment for Queen Elizabeth II when she died was hard to come by. But she had been the first in a long line of monarchs to lay a wreath at the Garden of Remembrance, a memorial to the 1916 Easter Rising, where the British had executed James Connolly, Padraig (Patrick) Pearse, and others. The Queen had done her part to put the darkness of colonialism to rest.

Ireland healed; Northern Ireland, not so much.

It's also easy to see how desperation shaped non-political aspects of the Irish culture. Oppressed people often look to divine sources for salvation and escape. Mysticism and strict devotion to Celtic energy and connectedness to their surroundings gave rise to an intangible power the stern Brits could not touch. This aspect of the Irish culture would grow to play an essential role in the spirituality that evolved as I explored my earthly limitations at altitude, time and again.

Sadly, in a case of can't-beat-em-join-em, a significant portion of my family tree became overly enamored with British culture and royalty. My Aunt Dorothy served with Queen Elizabeth II in World War II, wanted to be recognized as a Dame, and moved to London to raise her children. The palace did not award her that distinction. Despite the proximity, there was little interest in my maternal relatives to step foot on Irish soil. All of them essentially became British because it was advantageous to do so.

I found myself quite the opposite. My Fourteener quest magnetized me to the land. Project Children magnetized me to the land of my mother. As it turned out, after struggle comes peace.

Four years after the tragedy of 9/11, Curtis wanted to try another Fourteener.

To camp, I selected the La Garita Wilderness, part of the San Juan Mountain Range that gave us access to San Luis Peak. As the most remote of all the Fourteeners, it took much of the day to reach the trail head, including thirty miles of national forest road. We built a nice campfire and rested for the six-mile trek the following day.

San Luis is a low-risk, straightforward trail comprised of a few creek crossings, the occasional moose sighting, and many wide open bald-face meadows and rock fields. The mountain's elevation gain is only thirty-six hundred feet. It was one of the easier peaks left on my list, so I believed it would be perfect for Curtis.

At tree line, Curtis's breathing became noticeably labored. He stopped several times to catch his breath.

"Man, I don't know why I'm having such a hard time making it up this trail." His words pushed around his exhales with the aplomb of a sagging balloon.

"You just came from sea level." Explaining it away as the go-to reason in these parts—altitude—kept the more unpalatable alternatives from creeping to the forefront of my mind. Many first responders who had been at Ground Zero were beginning to show signs of cancer and lung ailments. Curtis and I knew each other's fitness levels like the laces on our well-worn boots. This was not like him.

"Why don't I go to the summit and meet you back at the trailhead?"

"I guess that's okay. I don't want to quit, but I don't want to slow you down."

So, at thirteen thousand feet, we parted. An hour later, I summited, snapped photos so Curtis could still enjoy the views, and then sat on a rock to recharge. I tried not to think about what held him back. Altitude, I told myself. I had only just rediscovered him in my life.

I was just about to make my descent when I spotted Curtis slowly making his way to the summit. At some points, he crawled on his hands and knees, but he didn't quit. My throat closed like a vice. My body was spent, but it still conspired every bit of residual energy toward one end: tears. Wind wicked them away as fast as they washed out the scenery. His determination exhilarated me.

San Luis was Curtis's last Fourteener. When he returned to Virginia, a respiratory check confirmed that he was losing his lung capacity. His prognosis was a gradual drop in function until he required oxygen. It was time to face the ramifications he knew would come from breathing in asbestos, polychlorinated biphenyls (PCBs), pulverized glass, and concrete at the World Trade Center collapse site.

Curtis and I often sought campsites miles into the forest, removed from others. Good views and solitude were our primary criteria. One dawn, in the Flat Tops Wilderness, at the edge of a ten-thousand-foot canyon and through a low fog, helicopter blades chopped the thin air, first at a distance, then increasingly louder and closer. In our bleary-eyed state, suspended between sleep and wakefulness, we stumbled from our tent, our stomachs knotted from the ambush.

The din rose from the valley floor, so close, until the copter burst into view a few hundred yards from us. It was a Blackhawk—no doubt, special forces training in adverse terrain. The pilot displayed exemplary skill where there were no visuals. Within seconds, the machine had diced the atmosphere and disappeared, no evidence it had been there, save our memories.

Curtis and I exchanged glances and shrugged. A bird of war in a serene place made us question if we were still zipped into our nylon sleeping bags, dreaming.

The helicopter remained a third party to our camping trip. Curtis grew increasingly affected and melancholy, reflecting on the part of him that had remained a firefighter long after he hung up his Kevlar coat with *Massey* stenciled on the back. He missed the comradery and the action.

Around the campfire that evening, he waded through the darker smoke of memories. He recounted the story of Frank and Johnny, two friends he served with in the Chesapeake, Virginia Fire Department. A blazing roof had collapsed on them, and they were found in the cinders with their arms wrapped around each other.

Curtis wept. I shifted closer and put an arm around his shoulders while he fell apart.

He had left the department three years before they died in 1994 to start his business. Yet, all these years later, the rawness of their deaths hung like a toxic cloud. He wanted to rewrite history, to have remained in the department on the day of that call. As it turned out, much of the blame fell on incompetent leadership at the scene. Curtis believed that by remaining a few more years, he could have prevented their deaths.

The stories did not stop. There were the two children missing in a house fire. Curtis had crawled on his hands and knees, searching and feeling around in the smoke-filled bedroom but couldn't find them. Only after the team had controlled the blaze and reentered the house did Curtis find the deceased children huddled beneath the bed against a wall. And there was a fellow firefighter who stepped between two uncoupled rail cars being recoupled. A connector went straight through his body. As Curtis and his comrades gathered around him, he asked for a final smoke and said, "Tell my wife and kids I love them." The front train car lurched ahead, exsanguinating his body.

Curtis had learned to compartmentalize trauma. It wasn't that he didn't trust the viability of his memories after all these years; he had distanced himself with a Kevlar layer of self-preservation. But the traumas never really go away. They hide in the smoke and fog, under the heaviness of moving pieces we shift in our lives, until life moves us forward.

I cannot say if this is the way, this exaggerated and conditioned tendency for humans to suppress it all. Holding a man who breaks in the healing amphitheater of nature opened me to our absolute thirst for belonging and connectedness and the necessity for replenishing from everything life's stresses steal from us. Holding a brother who does the same was a gift of mindful clarity, an awareness of living in the moment while holding space for all we had endured, separately and together.

Curtis's fellow first responders had all developed long-lasting coughs and shortness of breath, followed by complex cancers and respiratory diseases that could not be cured. It would take nine years before Congress would appropriate funds for the World Trade Center Health Program, called the James Zadroga 9/11 Health and Compensation Act, named in honor of an NYPD detective who was one of the first responders to contract a lung disease and die less than five years later. Due to Republican opposition in 2010, led by Senator Mitch McConnell, the legislation had stalled in the Senate. As part of his pledge to make President Obama a one-term president, McConnell had blocked important legislation at every turn.

Public outcry grew louder as Comedy Central's Jon Stewart castigated them on television for withholding funds so they could ensure an extension of a Bush-era corporate tax cut due to expire. Fifty-seven thousand people who qualified to begin receiving medical care and regular monitoring would get nothing. Political pressure finally forced McConnell to allow the support to be approved.

But after a few years, the fund was running out of money. Congress again refused to act until a House Judiciary hearing was called. Attending was Luis Alvarez, another first responder who appeared with Jon Stewart. "I will not stand by and watch as my friends with cancer from 9/11, like me, are valued less than anyone else because of when they get sick. You made me come here the day before my 69th round of chemo. I'm going to make sure that you never forget to take care of the 9/11 responders." Less than three weeks later, Alvarez died at the age of 53.

Curtis was reluctant to enroll in the program. He believed others needed the care and funds far more than he. Eventually, he realized the expertise this type of care required surpassed his ability to handle his diagnosis alone.

In 1998, ProPublica published an article referring to a former OSHA employee email sent to higher management: *"Just received a sample taken at the WTC (in or near the plume I believe), the result was very high ... EPA is saying it is one of the highest levels they have ever seen."* The level was almost one thousand times higher than normal for dioxin. It took fifteen years for the former head of the EPA, Christine Todd Whitman, to finally admit she was wrong to tell the public that post-9/11 air was safe. The federal government chose to portray the danger level as much lower, to sacrifice the health of some for the greater good of the whole. With the aloofness of a chess player, those in power often watch the slaughter of pawns from a hilltop. Or as Shakespeare wrote, *As flies to wanton boys are we to th' gods: They kill us for their sport.*

And so, Curtis and I climbed in honor of those lost, in honor of those whose service to others cost them dearly. As was our routine for long hikes, we brought small bottles of *sake* to toast the summit but also to toast being together and being alive. Ascent had become so much more than checkmarks on a list. Ascent was pushing limits in the ways that mattered, enduring the false summits inside ourselves, and looking for divine sources of salvation and escape.

Culebra Peak 14,047'

Chapter Nine

Ascending mountains and then looking back at them causes you to be reflective. Eight years earlier, our first hosted child, eleven-year-old Kelly Toal, came from a single-family home in the Catholic Nationalist area of Belfast called New Lodge. Kelly had long, dark hair and a warm smile, a rare treasure, given her shy disposition. Her father was not part of her life in any active sense. A few times that summer, we received calls from Kelly's mother, usually at three in the morning—ten a.m. in Ireland. Her slushy, drunken slurs on a thick brogue made deciphering her words nearly impossible.

For Kelly to leave home must have taken equal courage and guilt. Without her to buffer the darkness, her baby sister was left in the hands of their alcoholic mother, who had no husband around for support. During Kelly's stay, I often wondered if I, at eleven, with an unstable father and younger siblings to protect, could have made the same choice if given the opportunity. Would my mother have sent me off to strangers more than four thousand miles away? Would she have fretted about the host family taking in her son—*were they kind? Trustworthy?*

But Kelly came from a war zone—an added layer of distress. Parents put aside their worries because they knew spending a peaceful summer in America was the chance of a lifetime.

Being new to the hosting experience, we hadn't realized how lonely and fearful it was to give Kelly her own room to sleep in. Her first two nights, she was distraught and miserable from the nightly isolation. She was accustomed to having a sibling or family member beside her. When our eight-year-old daughter, Erin, offered to welcome Kelly into her bed, Kelly transitioned to being a bubbly and talkative girl.

On her first morning with us, and for several mornings after, Kelly quietly and right properly asked, "De'ya mind if I borrow an iron and board far ma clothes?" She wanted to present herself in the best light. Her garments were threadbare, barely holding up under the iron's heat. We took her on a shopping trip to a modest big-box store under the guise of finding play outfits so she didn't ruin the pretty ones she'd brought from home.

Soon, Erin and Kelly became inseparable. They giggled until late each night, played a nightly game of flashlight tag with the neighborhood kids, splashed around at the community pool, and pushed swings in the backyard. It was 1998, an idealized summer of peace in America until our innocence was taken by the Columbine tragedy the following spring.

For my daughter, Erin, this began the many-year joy of welcoming a new friend she had yet to meet, anxiously asking, "Who's coming this year, Daddy?" Many children would leave us with lasting and wonderful memories over the years, but Kelly would remain in my mind in a special way. She was our first Project Children child; she had our hearts.

Three years later, I knocked on the door at Kelly's New Lodge, Belfast home. She had made the front page of the Irish News.

Now, I understood what living in a conflict zone meant.

And I was afraid.

During Kelly's summer, *The Broomfield Enterprise* sent a journalist to a host family gathering. She wrote a newspaper article about Project Children's Colorado contingent entitled "Break from Belfast." The two-page feature presented a wonderful summary of the cause for peace and how the four initial children I had placed with host families were enjoying their summer. Pairing children of one faith with host families of a different faith had been a deliberate, risky choice, but it proved a success in bridging perceived differences. The article even quoted Neil, the Bedford's new son: "It's very nice here. The family has been good to me so far."

The article would prove fortuitous in my Irish journey.

Shortly after the article was published, I received a call from a man whose baritone voice sounded like he was from Northern Ireland. He introduced himself as Tom Quinn Kumpf, a Boulder-based photojournalist working on a book about children in conflict in Northern Ireland. He had recently returned from the war zone and read the article. He asked if he could meet the hosted children, show them some of his photographs, and learn about their experiences. I invited him to our going-away picnic.

Tom impressed me from our first encounter. He was a stocky, bearded man with an effortless smile and a warm disposition despite all he'd been through. After his time served in Vietnam, he traveled to conflict-ridden parts of the world, such as the former Soviet Union and Somalia, took what he observed about the then little-known Post Traumatic Stress Disorder (PTSD) present in himself and his fellow veterans, and began to wonder how the condition might manifest in children, especially when they had no means of escaping ongoing trauma. How did they adapt? While seeing and experiencing war, could the innocence with which they entered the world still be found or even renewed?

Tom's working-class Pittsburgh-based Irish roots proved a natural fit for our hosted children. They gathered around him to see his photographs. In his subject matter, some of the four kids recognized a soccer coach, their neighborhood, a teacher, or a brother's best friend. These micro-connections were joyful and made it easy for the children to open up to him and share about their lives back home. At the time, his project was little more than spiral-bound notes and evocative black-and-white images.

His book, independently published a few years later, was titled *Children of Belfast* and became widely recognized as a moving account of how children, at an early age, acquire the *thousand-yard stare*. Written with a poignant ability to highlight comic observation while in the saddest of circumstances, Tom was told that, "The Protestants hide their kids away when the journalists come around, or their kids just won't talk, while the Catholics, hell, every one of them seems to be born with the bloody PR skills." Tom also described kneecapping, a means of enforcing the rules of a local paramilitary. If a young person was caught drug dealing or joy riding (stealing a car), they would be brought to a place of judgment. A small caliber pistol would be placed behind the knee, and the trigger pulled, blowing out the kneecap. For the rest of their lives, many would carry the stigma of having this done and easily recognized as they walked with a limp. The book had a poignant dedication: "To my daughters, Lisa and Erin, and to all children who, only by virtue of their birth, suffer the consequences of violence and war."

A few years later, Tom published a large coffee table book, *Ireland, Standing Stones to Stormont*, which won the travel essay category of the Ben Franklin Award from the National Independent Book Publishers (NIBP). Tom invited me to the award presentation in New York. It was an honor to see someone so talented recognized for his work. We had become friends. After the picnic with Tom and the Irish children, I introduced him to Denis Mulcahy, the chairman and face of Project Children, where Tom made further connections that elevated awareness of his book. Increased sales helped him recover from the financial hardships of getting the book to market without sponsorship and brought him deserved recognition as a gifted writer and photographer.

Watching him stand at the podium to accept his award at the New York banquet, I craved an escalation of my Irish connection. No longer was it enough to host children. To move forward into the fullness of who I was meant to become, I had to go back.

I leaned toward Tom and said, "Ever thought about being a chaperone to a jumbo airliner full of Irish kids?"

Culebra, Spanish for *serpent*, was my only summit that summer. The Fourteener is the highest privately-owned peak in the world. From the aspen-lined groves at the trailhead to the snake-like twists at the ridgeline, it is a hike loaded with vegetation, wildlife, undefined trails for the roamers at heart, and, at the top, remarkable views of Red Mountain and the other peaks in the Culebra range.

At this point in my quest, I was beginning to redefine beauty. Certainly, I had lived where nature reigned supreme in my mind. England is hedgerows and farms. Maine is sharp coastlines and expansive forests. Virginia is rolling hills and isolated marshlands. These locations held a sort of arrested beauty, where I had to look harder past the human footprint to tap into nature's rhythms. My business travels had taken me all over the world, but the polarity of the two places of my heart aligned with very different notions of beauty.

There is a reason that Colorado's grandeur is the subject of paintings by artists from Thomas Moran and Albert Bierstadt to William Henry Holmes and Georgia O'Keefe. In Colorado's high country, every angle is art. Every trail is tangibly surreal. The people of the state have made concerted efforts to push back against the human footprint, cognizant of how overdevelopment might subtract from an area's vibrancy.

In truth, I was drawn to the mountains for the visual clutter of humankind that it subtracted. I was further drawn to the Fourteener peaks because the summits were an even more enhanced version of this ideal. The effort required to get to these vistas made the views more spectacular. There is a mantra in mountaineering—*Leave it as you find it*. I'd go so far as to say, *Leave it better than you found it*. I'm still astounded by the ways that hikers defile the land. But I so chased the pristine messiness of nature that even the canisters left by park services at the Fourteener summits did not sit right with me. It was evidence of man that defied our unspoken promise to the earth. Those who felt the need to write their names on the list or shove artifacts inside were climbing to leave a mark, the ultimate expression of ego. It's impossible *not* to fall in love with Colorado's beauty; those who are present enough to appreciate and respect it see its true gifts.

Not entirely in contrast, Ireland is breathtaking. Certainly, as a smaller slice of earth, it contains more human footprints. It is a landscape of extreme comfort—worn slippers, a favorite tonic landing on the belly, glowing embers on a cool night. But it is also alive with energy. Historical places often are. They carry residual emotion of those who've come before. The collective energy in Ireland is otherworldly, mystical, wise, a bit playful at times, and never far from a haunting message.

I craved that message with every lost element inside me. As it turned out, both places of the heart had something important to say.

In recent decades, attempts at citizen-staged peace movements have met with moderate success. Liberia's non-violent movement, led by activist Leyman Gbowee, brought Muslim and Christian women together with the aim of ending the fourteen-year civil war. Similarly, women in Nicaragua and El Salvador have stood for the end to civil unrest. And in 1989, Belgian activist Simone Sussland helped to convene the first-ever women's peace conference aimed at the conflict between Israel and Gaza. These movements met with admirable and moderate success in moving the collective toward more understanding and tolerance.

However, these were adults trying to convince adults, a much harder prospect than reaching the minds and hearts of individuals who haven't yet settled into their prejudices and biases. Pre-teens and early teens are malleable. They are not born with hatred in their hearts, so it made sense that to bring lasting peace to a region, impulses toward understanding and tolerance must begin before the darkness of the isms, before first-hand experiences darken the prospects of peace. Reach the boys before they become instruments of war; reach the girls who push forward compassion in any society.

The window of opportunity is narrow: mature enough for international travel, young enough to have not fallen into the indoctrination of hatred.

At its inception, the founders of Project Children could not have realized such a peace potential was possible. In the 1970s, nothing like Project Children yet existed inside any other political conflict on the globe. Denis and the founders simply wanted to reach behind them, to cultivate the favor that Americanization had brought into their lives, and save a few kids from violence.

They could not have realized the generational trauma they healed, the politicians who began to listen to the Project Children's testimonials, and that their gesture of goodwill, an attempt to eradicate violence in the hearts of the most oppressed children, would bring lasting peace to Northern Ireland.

So where did Project Children succeed where other similar movements had only met with modest success?

An essential component of the program's eventual achievement was the diaspora of displaced Irish in America. It wasn't a movement that incorporated displaced Irish around the globe; it was a tight group of highly motivated recent immigrants who were already supporting each other in all the ways they could. New York and the eastern seaboard, a thick enclave of recent and more removed generations from the homeland, became a natural foundation for such a movement. Denis and the founders of Project Children plugged into the organic network of Irish who populated the police and fire departments, a natural camaraderie and the Irish credo of caring for one's own.

This was Project Children's opening stage. Four children. That was all. Four children, half Catholic and half Protestant, that founders and host families hoped to love and nourish into a space of tolerance and open-mindedness. Those four had a life-altering experience and the two communities so impacted—that little town of Greenwood Lake in America and the neighborhoods in Belfast—heard of such love and wanted to be part of something special. Every subsequent summer, the love and affection spread like a contagion of goodwill. Several years in, with the numbers who wanted to participate on either side of the pond exploding, Project Children's founders realized what they had on their hands. Something greater than the original intent. Something greater than themselves.

Something that had the potential to, over time, solve the problem of sectarian violence in Northern Ireland. Children who befriend those they are told to hate grow into adults who no longer wish to carry hatred for those they befriended.

I understood this ballooning sentiment because it was precisely what I witnessed when I facilitated Project Children in Colorado. Four children to start. That was all. For our part, our family loved our host children. We wanted them back year after year, and we wanted new children as well. The momentum of shared love strung my summers together in a way that only the mountains touched for me.

I was ordinary. Forgettable in every way, in all stages of life. But I was part of a peace movement that took a pent-up need and released a valve of hope. I flowed right along with the children who craved harmony, stability, tranquility.

Eight years on, our family decided to take a break from hosting a child with Project Children. Though five other children were placed in other Colorado host families, my daughter, Erin, now fifteen, wanted to see what it was like to welcome one of the Aer Lingus flights to New York and join me in escorting them to Colorado. When the plane pulled up to the hangar under an arc of green and orange water sprayed from two fire trucks, she teared up, same as me. As a reward for her welcoming heart over the years, I arranged that summer to fly her to Ireland to visit two of the girls from Newry and Lurgan we had previously hosted.

Though there was still no functioning government in Northern Ireland seven years after the signing of the Good Friday Agreement, the IRA finally committed to disarming and placing their weapons beyond verifiable use. It was looking to be one of the most peaceful years in memory. For Erin, it was the chance of a lifetime. She came home changed, with a broader worldview and more appreciation of the peaceful world she had grown up in.

That hope carried into our family's ninth summer of involvement with Project Children. Eight children came to Colorado. Like many involved in the peace effort, I held my breath. Coordinators were anxious to see the long-desired goal of lasting peace finally realized. But when it was discovered that the British military had colluded with local Protestant paramilitaries to target Irish Republicans and kill them in the campaign to defeat the IRA, trust was severely shaken. On May 15th, 2006, Northern Ireland's political parties were given six months to develop a power-sharing government or sovereignty would revert indefinitely back to the British government. Pressure only increased on the two factions when it was announced that British troops would be withdrawn by the following August as part of the commitment to the Good Friday Agreement.

The political climate made it an important year for Tom and me to visit Ireland together. In our respective ways, we had attempted to make a difference in the lives of Northern Ireland's children. Tom's second book, *Ireland: Standing Stones to Stormont*, transported me. Weaving the most memorable blend of photography and storytelling I had ever read—and reread and reread—I longed for encounters with the locals. I wanted to experience their connection with ring forts on a hill, standing stones in a field, and fairy trees that must never be cut to avoid bad luck. The book gave me a sense of two coexisting worlds of Ireland's terrain: struggle and mystical remembrance.

The book's backbone highlighted healing wells cared for by a woman in the village until the caretaker died and responsibility passed to the next woman in the family. Feminine hereditary lines of caretaking often stretch back hundreds of years. In some circumstances, when the tradition was to bring a well's healing water to the afflicted, if the caretaker had passed and there was no heir, the Irish awaited decisions made by the *sidhe*, pronounced *she*.

The fairy folk.

In all ways, *Standing Stones to Stormont* was a literary transport to the Celtic otherworld of *Tir na nOg*, the Land of Eternal Youth. As a storyteller, a true mystic whose travels had ingratiated him to those who believed, Tom became the land's ultimate guide.

And I was never the same.

Once all two hundred and fifty children were properly received from their Aer Lingus flight from New York to Dublin and guided to waiting buses to take them home to Belfast and other towns north, Tom and I began a tour of his second book.

We rented a car and drove two hours to our first stop in Northern Ireland, the Neolithic site of *Ahvin Maha*, Emain Macha, in County Armagh. As one of the most cited places in ancient Irish literature, Emain Macha's ruling dynasty and traditions date back to the fourth through seventh centuries BC. The site consists of roundhouses and enclosures sunk into the landscape and revered as the political and social capital of its time. Tom advised that we should approach counterclockwise to pay respects to the sacredness of the locale.

The warm summer day brought out many people to savor the sunshine. Children rolled down the hill while parents clustered on the hilltops to talk. Tom pointed out two oak trees at the base of the mound. In *Standing Stones to Stormont*, the same oaks had sheltered him from a storm. I studied the horizon. A dark band of clouds neared. In minutes, the winds kicked up.

Tom laughed. "She likes me."

People scurried back to their cars and places of shelter, unseen. Soon, Tom and I were the only ones around.

Beneath the oaks, as the storm arrived, we gripped the lapels of our jackets closed. Rain pelted the sacred hills. I sat with my back to the grand trunk of one while behind me a bit, Tom reclined against the other. The storm swelled with intensity. The wind shrieked, and droplets raced sideways and up and diagonally, seemingly wrestling with itself in which direction to go. I marveled at the display before me. At that moment, a powerful feminine energy entered my awareness. It seemed to emanate from the tree supporting my weight. The energy was sensual and welcoming.

I felt an embrace.

And I startled.

Tom snored softly over my shoulder. His relaxed state was almost a permission to close my eyes and sink deeper into whatever the moment brought. Cautiously, I relived the sensation of the hug, warm and calm and so at odds with the chaos of nature surrounding us.

Time ran in rivulets down the land. For thirty minutes, maybe thirty years, I reveled in my sacred experience at Emain Macha. Was I predisposed to sense this? Was this my heritage welcoming me home?

Eventually, a more distant thunderclap awoke Tom. We gathered ourselves from the land and left the spot. Tom said nothing, just smiled as if to say, *See? I told you this shit is real.*

The next day, in Belfast, Tom and I ventured into the inner sanctum of an Irish Republican neighborhood and the home of Catherine Hamill. In 1995, at age nine, she read a welcome letter to President Bill Clinton, the first sitting U.S. President to visit Northern Ireland.

Catherine lived with her mother, Laura Hamill, and her stepfather, a former IRA man who had attempted to kill a British soldier and had spent ten years in prison as a result. When she was an infant, her father had been killed by Protestant paramilitaries who burst into their home and shot him in his chair. Her letter summarized the hope of all children living in war-torn Northern Ireland: *I live in Belfast. I love where I live. My first daddy died in the Troubles. It was the saddest day of my life. I still think of him. Now it is nice and peaceful. I like having peace and quiet for a change instead of people shooting and killing. My Christmas wish is that peace and love will last in Ireland forever.*

As we left, I shook the hand of Catherine's stepfather and discovered he was missing two fingers. In his attempt to shoot the British soldier, wounding him in the neck, the return fire blew off those fingers. For the first time, I understood Tom's special skill in being welcomed into a cloistered world that few outsiders penetrated. By way of Vietnam, this veteran of Irish descent from Pittsburgh's south side was someone who had lived the burden of war and pulling the trigger. The Irish knew he understood their struggle.

A mural in West Belfast, painted in Irish and Basque languages, showed how interwoven the ideology for shaking off the bonds of an oppressor could be. The words roughly translated into *Two People, One Struggle* and to *Take Freedom*. As we drove out of the neighborhood, no street corner observers watched us as they had when we arrived.

We carved out a southwest path, to a part of Ireland I had never visited. Almost melancholy in its exquisiteness, and wind swept, with ring forts and standing stones so protected that we had to sometimes ask permission of the owner to visit them. I found it increasingly difficult to absorb everything I saw and was told. The otherworldliness paired with the myths and legends and Tom's vignettes felt hypnotic, almost dreamlike.

The Burren seemed more like the Alaskan tundra than Ireland. With miles of stone fences and an open landscape crowded with limestone, it was unlike any landscape I had seen in the Emerald Isle. Of the nine hundred native species of plants in the country, seventy percent are found in the Burren. Yet, the western part of Ireland had also seen the worst of the Potato Famine during the 1850s, as the soil was sparse and difficult to farm. In total, more than one million people—twenty percent of Ireland's population—died. Most were children. A hundred years before that, in 1740, between thirteen and twenty percent of the population had also starved to death due to an epic climate event that froze much of the country solid for months and destroyed grain and livestock.

Staring out at the Burren's unforgiving topography, I understood how such famine was possible.

We paid our respects at a memorial that depicted a steel panel door with a child leaning against it, hoping to be let inside. Another panel showed a letter written to superiors in London: *Gentlemen, there is a little boy named Michael Rice of Lahinch, aged about four years. He is an orphan, his father having died last year, and his mother has expired on last Wednesday night, who is now being buried without a coffin!! Unless ye make some provision as such. The child is now at the workhouse gate expecting to be admitted. If not, he will starve.* The marker was a grim introduction to this stark and painful chapter in the country's history.

Near Kilfenora, a town in County Clare that meant *church of the fertile hillside*, Tom deposited me at the bottom of a famine road.

"Take a walk," he instructed.

Intellectually, I understood these roads went nowhere. Now, he wanted me to experience one. As the starving Irish, unable to pay rent, lost their homes and farm plots and were evicted, many were forced to enter workhouses of the most horrific state. With typhus and dysentery rampant, those who could work were forced to take stones from the countryside to build these useless roads.

Deliberately, I ascended a gentle slope with a stone fence on one side and an open field on the other. The rocky landscape, remnants of ancient glacial terrain and *turlochs*—rainwater that collects into a lake then disappears with the shifting water table—unraveled so that Tom and the car disappeared from view. I entered the sacred space, imagining myself stacking and laying stones in the cold and driving rain, with hunger pangs in my belly such that I had never known. I came upon a fairy tree in the circle of a ring fort. Two wild goats, one black and one white, observed me from a distance.

I stopped.

In an instant, I was overcome with weakness. I collapsed against the stone fence and wept in gasping heaves. Feeling the loss of all those who had died, especially the children, my soul was no longer in the present. I had never felt more in turmoil or more at peace.

The transcendent experience weakened me so that I couldn't rise. I cannot say how long I remained on the ground. When I found the strength to stand, I walked the half-mile back, still in a trance-like state. Somehow, I had traveled beyond this plane of existence and returned to a locale that was hauntingly familiar. Somehow, in my lineage, I had circled back to a place I had always been.

At the car, Tom paced, his brow heavy with sharp angles.

"Where were you?"

His unexpected tone snapped me out of any lingering ethereal frame of mind. That I had upset him made me feel like the mud in my boot treads.

"You were gone so long, I thought you had fallen into a hole in the porous limestone. People do that here. They step atop something green and fall away, never to be heard from again. Entire canyons beneath the grass. Turn up years later, having been taken by the fairies underground. They find the world has journeyed on, but they haven't aged a day."

I nearly smirked at his response. Ever the storyteller, and with such conviction toward the fantastical. After my time near the stone wall, nothing he said seemed implausible. He had feared for my safety and felt responsible for my well-being. I could no more explain to him what I had experienced than I could put words to it myself. To share the sacredness of it all, I feared, was to diffuse its power. So I simply said, "Forgive me."

"I had wanted to make Lisdoonvarna. The Kaylee dance."

"I know. I shouldn't have stayed so long. It's just so beautiful."

Tom sighed, his earlier hive of displeasure seemingly dispensed on the breeze. "That it is."

I didn't want to leave, but we had more stops. Mists of the landscape carried us from one timeless place to another. Buried truths older than our physical bodies surfaced in our remote memories—at once reachable and intangible. My heart continued to open with each new kilometer.

Certainly, the years of bringing children out of conflict in Northern Ireland, learning their inherited stories and their present struggles, resonated with me. Facing the emotional wounds of the Irish children entrusted to me had resurfaced my childhood wounds. At times, merely watching the children arrive or talking through a special memory with a Project Children participant choked me up, sometimes in the most embarrassing times and places. I didn't understand it; I didn't suppress it. I recognized its healing properties and allowed its inevitability to flow through me.

Ireland, though, was different. It was as if the universe said, *I see you, Anthony. Here is even more.*

It was no longer their journey but mine.

El Diente 14,159'

Chapter Ten

The last stretch on El Diente is narrow and loose. And the sky had unleashed wave after wave of brute force: high winds, temperature drop, horizontal snow. Simultaneous lightning flashes and thunder claps. I scrambled down and aimed for the nearest large outcropping. My hands shook. A churning fog of gray and white smothered everything within sight.

My cell phone had twelve percent battery and one bar.

I bit off my glove and slid my fingers across the keypad. I pressed it to my ear.

"State police, what's your emergency?" came a man's voice.

I pushed my voice past my collapsed throat, hard. Hard enough to be heard past the howling winds.

"Anthony Massey." I stated my home phone number, for Darlene, should the signal be lost and I died, so that she could be properly notified. "I'm on El Diente…near the summit…the storm. I need help."

"I'll transfer you to the closest search and rescue. Hang on, Anthony. We'll get you help."

Warm tears gathered. The wind wicked them free.

The call silenced—twenty seconds, thirty seconds. My hands quaked so hard I feared I would send the phone sailing off the cliff. *Oh god…it dropped.* I glanced at the screen, what I could see of it. It had not returned to a home screen.

A new voice gargled through the phone. I pressed it to my ear. "Hello?"

"Anthony, this is … and rescue …know that mountain well… describe …where you are."

I shouted details of my predicament, pausing only when the rumbles of thunder overpowered any hope of him hearing me.

"…doing great, Anth…I know exactly … are. Can you retrace….?"

"Ridge is thick with snow. Zero visibility," I hollered. "Impossible."

"Can you…couloir below…?"

"No." Snow buried the route.

The voice did not come as it had been—consistent and strong.

The call dropped. I lost him. Oh god, oh god, oh god.

"Anthony?"

I had never liked the sound of my name until that utterance.

"… take the opposite side of the ridge…sending a team…meet you … keep descending. Don't. Stop. Okay?"

No helicopter. Not in these conditions. Survival was on me.

Before I hung up, he said, "See you soon."

See you soon. Such confidence, when I had none.

I zipped the phone back into my jacket and gloved my hand again. The alternate route's descent was nothing more than guesswork. The mountain was steep and slippery, and the clouds obscured everything below. Given my limited visibility, cliffing out—stuck with no way down and no means to climb back up—was a persistent threat. I dropped from one ledge to another, playing out each move in my head before executing. *Was right or left better? If I drop to that ledge, then what?* I guessed and second-guessed each move, a crippling exercise in self-doubt. Snowfall accumulation at an unbelievable rate made it hard to gauge if a ledge's angle was stable or too slick to land.

One wrong step, and I would slide off into oblivion.

After one slip and recovery, my internal voice pleaded with the universe. *Let me live one more day. Please. Just one more.*

Wayne and I had been hiking together for four previous summers when I got a call from him. He wanted desperately to get back on a Fourteener. "Let's do the three in the Sangre De Cristo range." He went on to explain that he wanted me to drive his truck up the access road because he thought I was ready to handle a "real" four-wheel drive road. Maybe he thought it would convince me to get rid of my station wagon. Wayne also had a suspended driver's license for a recent DUI, but where we were going, there wouldn't be a police officer manning a sobriety checkpoint. I hesitated for a second or two and then agreed.

"I'm in. And as Dustin Hoffman said in *Rain Man*, 'I'm a very good driver.'"

Lake Como Road is one of the toughest four-wheel drive roads in America. Attempt it with a passenger car or SUV, and you might as well call your insurance company to report the self-inflicted damage before you set out. Out of curiosity and overconfidence in my family wagon, I once tested how far up Lake Como Road it would take me. A mile or two in, I encountered rocks the size of my wheels. Truly impossible, I thought, for *any* vehicle.

Many climbers park their cars at the base of the road near the Sand Dunes and hike up the four thousand feet to reach the lake and set up base camp. But hiking the road is no picnic, either. Large rocks and the southwest summer sun angle make for a long and hot hike through the scrub oak.

Neither choice to get to Lake Como was easy.

I struggled in that conversation to find words. That we had bonded enough to put our lives in each other's hands on a Fourteener, but he hadn't told me he was serving time, that he wanted to launch back into our partnership with a five-mile stretch at 11,700 feet that was treacherous, and I'd be driving—it all seemed too much.

I invited Craig Huey, my hiking partner from my first Fourteener, Mount Princeton, to help share the four-hour drive from home. We met Wayne at Walsenburg, where his mother had driven him in his truck with plans for a friend to take her back to Raton, New Mexico. At the Great Sand Dunes National Park, we picked up the desert-floor portion of Lake Como Road. Wayne was beside me in the passenger seat; Craig sat in the truck bed.

The short pinion pine and rocks became larger boulders and hairpin turns. At a 180-degree switchback we estimated to be the final mile or two, facing a scary-steep grade with huge rocks blocking the path, I said, "I'm not comfortable with this, driving your truck. If you want us to keep going, you'll have to drive."

Wayne and Craig hopped out of the truck and moved the larger rocks off the road. I waited in the truck. Wayne began approaching the driver's side to take over. I put on the emergency brake and shifted the truck to neutral, paused a moment to ensure everything held, then exited the vehicle. I gently closed the driver's side door.

The emergency brake failed.

Immediately, the truck rolled backward. Instinctively I grabbed onto the doorframe. Under normal conditions, I might have been able to hold it, but the steep grade and gravity dragged me backwards so fast, my heels skipped over the substantial road rocks. I held on a handful of yards before I let go. The four-thousand-pound vehicle careened down the road and off the side of the mountain.

It somersaulted twice, spewing our gear out of the back, and dis-appeared from view.

The valley quieted.

We stood in silence, none of us daring to speak.

Had Wayne not gotten out to pick up rocks, had Craig not hopped out of the bed, the outcome might have been tragic. I was certain Wayne would want to take a swing at me, so I didn't make eye contact.

"Wayne, I'll do whatever I can to replace your truck."

He said nothing.

We climbed down the slope to see what remained of the truck. Backpacks, sleeping bags, and other gear littered the hillside. The truck was upright, its engine still running. The cab was crushed to oblivion. We turned off the engine, salvaged what we could, and hiked down the road with what we could carry. At mile three, we set up camp, returned to the crash site to retrieve the rest of our gear, and removed the license plates at Wayne's request—"It's so remote and steep, it'll never be discovered," he said—and made our way back to camp. Exhaustion had set in, and my big toe was bleeding from having been run over by the truck tires and then hiking on it all day. At the lower elevation, I called home. I needed Darlene to come get Craig and me and take us back to Walsenburg so I could get my wagon.

The loss of Wayne's truck was a mixed bag of luck. I provided seventy percent of the funds to replace his truck—all I could manage—but the financial hardship on him merely added to his woes. Bad luck, however, turned out to be the motivation he needed to address his drinking for good. He enrolled in treatment and counseling, took a deep interest in yoga, became a yoga instructor, and remained sober.

A year after our Lake Como Road adventure, Wayne received a call from the U.S. Forest Service. They had used the Vehicle Identification Number (VIN) to track the ownership back to Wayne. Their directive: get it out or pay a massive fine. It cost two thousand dollars to remove the truck. I cobbled together what funds I could to help with the removal. The skill and equipment required to get the truck up on the road and back to the salvage yard were impressive. The wrecker company's money was well earned.

Wayne's seventy-year-old mother was a saint. Over the next couple of years, while he waited to earn his license back, she drove him to where we would meet at a trailhead to hike a mountain. After setting up camp for us, she slept in the seat of her Subaru with a blanket and waited for us to return. She and Wayne would then drive home. She knew climbing was good therapy for Wayne and her best way of supporting him. That support, and mountaineering, made all the difference. More than fifteen years later, he hasn't had another drink.

The ones who love us and support this bizarre thirst to summit peaks deserve recognition equal to those who take the physical steps. Golf widows deal with the expense and Saturday afternoons spent on an 18-hole course; Mountain widows lose us for days-long stretches and catalog our trips to the emergency room. When we are with them, we are thinking of the hikes to come. We travel tremendous distances, inconvenience them when we make errors in judgment, and spend a king's ransom on expensive gear to keep us from freezing to death. Our loved ones say, "So long"—not goodbye, never goodbye—never knowing if they'll get a phone call from a stranger that will shatter their lives.

It was six years before Wayne and I found ourselves on Lake Como Road again. Wayne had his license back by then, and I was nearing the end of my quest—four Fourteeners left, three of which were up this difficult road.

An hour after search and rescue severed the call, I reached El Diente's drainage region. I picked my way over a large and loose boulder field toward the distant tree line. My right ankle rolled on a rock.

Searing pain shot up my leg. I paused to catch my breath through gritted teeth. Putting weight on it proved excruciating. My fatigue had finally bested me into lazy steps. From my backpack, I withdrew an extra sock. I stuffed one into my right boot and cinched the laces as tight as possible to provide support. I hobbled on, wondering, realistically, how far I could make it on what I was sure was a broken ankle.

As darkness fell, a distant flashlight came into view. One man with an identifying coat.

Search and rescue.

I made it. Twelve hours after I had set out solo, I was safe.

My knees turned liquid. I nearly collapsed with relief, but no part of me wanted any delay in getting off the mountain. I staggered and waved and shouted like a madman. When we reached each other, he shook my hand and told me his name. I was too dazed and exhausted to remember it.

"I was about to turn around when I saw you," he said.

"Thank you," I managed.

"Sure thing. Let's get you down and warm."

"I've hurt my ankle."

"I got you, man."

My rescuer was young, vibrant, and strong. He looped my spaghetti arms around his neck and hefted me onto his back. A few steps into the return trek, his breath labored. My limbs overpowered his shorter frame like a gangly albatross.

"How about I lean on you?" I suggested.

He gave an easy chuckle. "That would probably be faster."

Shortly after, we met up with the rest of the team. Another rescuer propped me up on the other side. At the all-terrain vehicle driven to the trailhead, they piled me on and drove me to the S&R truck. I gratefully accepted a ride back to my campsite, not realizing it would be a circuitous two-hour drive back. My bearings were disoriented, and I was numb with exhaustion. The vehicle cab warmed me to my core. They informed me they were from the nearby town of Rico—which gave me an odd sense of synergy because my employer was the Japanese company, Ricoh.

"You have a hiker's insurance card?" asked the team lead.

"No. What's that?"

"Keeps you from being charged for search and rescue. Thousands of dollars."

The only thing that took my mind off my ankle pain was the potential pain to my wallet. I promised him I would purchase the insurance as soon as I got home.

I never received a bill from Rico's S&R.

Back at my campsite, sitting in my car, I worked on releasing the tension and exhaustion from my shoulders. My phone rang.

Darlene.

With all the positive, don't-worry-about-me energy I could summon, I answered.

She had been trying to reach me much of the evening to make sure I was okay. Darlene didn't typically check on me while I was on my hikes, but she had an uneasy feeling about my decision to do El Diente alone. I shared my ordeal with her.

"Do you like doing this to yourself?"

Her tone wasn't angry or bitter. In fact, she was downright therapeutic about it all. Lead the fool to the most logical end, then wait for him to sip of the absurdity. I had been reckless. More than one miscalculation. I felt six inches tall. No answer came.

That night, another storm pounded the area so hard that I couldn't justify climbing into my tent. I made the best of the situation by sleeping in the back of the wagon. I had no painkillers. My ankle kept me awake most of the night. But I was alive. And lucky—again.

The next morning, before driving out, I paused to glance at the ridge that had trapped me. Beautiful. Pristine. Snow-covered. Around me, the aspens had stepped into their glorious colors. I snapped a photo of where I almost lost my life. In my mind, I labeled the image *No Fond Farewell*. Had I not gotten off the mountain, I would have frozen to death. The previously forecasted cold front arrived as I drove home. Along the way, I stopped by the side of the road, limped out to stretch my muscles, and studied the dark line of clouds approaching from the west.

El Diente's storm that nearly froze me to death had generated locally. A freak thing, orographic uplift and such. Nearly impossible to forecast or prepare for. A mountaineer's nemesis: localized atmospheric conditions that change in a blink.

My ankle had sustained only a sprain. I was on crutches for two weeks until I had to fly to Chicago on business. While on a trip to the Great Lakes Naval Training Base for an appointment, a car rear-ended me and caused a chain accident with the car ahead of me. My seatbelt protected me from both impacts. The man at fault who rear-ended me pressed me for my insurance and contact information. He tried to rush me past the next steps of calling the authorities but failed. Police cited him at the scene. I drove on to my appointment and then to the airport to return the accordion car, crunched into little more than a boxy cabin. On the two-hour flight home, not yet fully recovered from my El Diente ordeal, with a reinjured ankle and a bruised chest from the seatbelt, I resolved to seek medical attention.

Because the car accident happened while I acted in a work capacity, I had to go through the intensive process of paperwork and red tape to seek treatment. I went back to crutches. And despite my complaining of a new cough, doctors assured me that my increasing chest pain was the result of the seatbelt impact and advised me to wait for the bruising to subside.

My condition worsened. In frustration, I drove to the nearby emergency room. Chest x-rays confirmed that I had pneumonia in both lungs. I suspected I had inhaled particles on that windy El Diente day, but surely what followed—the trauma of rescue, the compromised ankle, and the car accident—was simply too much for my body to overcome. My hiking was done for the year, and I was down in all ways for a month.

A fourth attempt of El Diente would have to wait.

Not long after my recovery, I received a subpoena from the Cook County District Attorney, requiring me to come to a court hearing regarding the accident. When I called to learn more, I learned that the person who hit me disputed the ticket, and if I didn't appear, he couldn't be convicted. I was incensed. I arranged travel back to Chicago and attended the hearing. The look on the guy's face was one of surprise. He must have been gambling that I wouldn't show up for the court hearing. The assistant DA read aloud the guy's past convictions—violations that ranged from numerous speeding violations to DUIs and, finally, leaving the scene of an accident *resulting in death*. After hearing the previous violations, the judge simply looked at the defendant and said, "So, I assume you will be pleading guilty?" I came out of the courtroom thankful I wasn't a worse victim.

Three months later, on December twenty-first, the Winter Solstice, feeling largely recovered from my traumas, I wanted to offer thanks to the universe for still being alive. I asked a friend to join me on a hike to the summit of the 8,400-foot Bear Peak. The two-hour hike went as planned until we arrived at the top. I pulled out two small bottles of champagne that I had placed in my backpack, with the intention to enjoy them as a toast, but it was so bitterly cold we couldn't drink them. We returned them to the pack, high-fived, and started down.

That evening, I put wood in a chimenea on my back porch and stared into the fire. The car accident had reinforced that life was short, that every time I climbed a Fourteener, I may have been asking for risk but that true risk was all around us, even on a high-traffic street in Chicago. At my last breath, I didn't want to be *the guy who attempted all the Fourteeners*. I wanted to be *the guy who climbed all the Fourteeners*—one of the oldest who ever attempted such an accomplishment. My quest had taken me to the edge, but I was too far gone to stop. I would climb El Diente and the remaining Fourteeners or die trying.

Seeing Wayne grounded in his new life as a sober man convinced me we should return in August 2007 to the Telluride area and make one final attempt at *The Tooth*. We were confident in the trail up to where Mount Wilson joined El Diente—he had hiked it twice, and, for me, it would be my fourth visit. But as we climbed higher, the route proved a formidable challenge. The massive ridge is steep; in several sections, the mountain is a near-vertical slope. The plan was to climb Mount Wilson and then take the back side of the ridge to El Diente's summit, but we soon realized that route would make for an extremely long day.

Together, we decided to go up one of the steep gulleys and remain along the periphery to find solid hand and foot holds, which allowed us to crest the top of the ridge where I had been trapped in the storm. This time, the weather was good, and we celebrated reaching the summit.

My god. All the miles, the pain, the mishaps. I had reached the top of one of Colorado's toughest mountains. Looking 360 degrees at what a few years earlier had been shrouded in clouds the day I called 9-1-1, in every direction were rugged, jagged mountains reaching thirteen or fourteen thousand feet. The San Juan mountains contain fourteen Fourteeners and three hundred and fourteen peaks that reach thirteen thousand feet. Climbers could spend the better part of life killing themselves on all the magnificence. The San Juans are not a playground for the faint of heart.

Shortly after reaching El Diente's peak, I discovered my water bladder had leaked and was almost empty. Dehydration would almost certainly lead to leg cramps, and we still had another four hours of return hike.

I took tiny sips of what water remained, acutely aware that a descent—on any mountain, but in particular the one I had previously failed three times—could be lethal. Wayne and I selected a more direct descent into a couloir facing the Navajo Basin drainage and downed it carefully. The route was steep and, in sections, loose scree was abundant. We attempted to keep to the periphery, as before, to maintain the best footing conditions, but eventually, they fizzled out, and we were forced to cross mid-gully. In that middle section, my feet went out from under me, and I slid.

I kept sliding.

And sliding.

And sliding.

I self-arrested on a passing rock. The debris field ripped flesh off my left leg from knee to upper thigh, but I had narrowly avoided the mountaineer's dreaded *long slide* of death. My heart nearly pounded free of my chest. The raw wound oozed and bled. Wayne had enough zinc oxide with him to stop the contents of my outer leg from running down my shins. The remainder of the descent was uneventful but painful. We stopped at a stream to replenish our drinking supply and add water treatment pills. The night in the tent was uncomfortable. For weeks afterward, I felt like one long, ugly scab. But, finally, El Diente had been climbed.

Not conquered. Climbed.

As I was nearing my last handful of Fourteeners, I had learned that climbers never really conquer mountains—they simply allow us to visit them. Sometimes they inject the fullness of life directly into our veins. Sometimes they arrest life or take it away altogether.

El Diente was such a peak: most capable of lessons, great and small, but also best left in the rearview mirror. Never had recording a peak's name in my hiking journal been so sweet.

Wayne's mother died of a heart attack. He was devastated. She had so supported his passion for mountaineering. Mightily, he held onto his sobriety, but he missed her companionship and often wished he had a woman in his life. A chance encounter with a bank teller opened the door for him to fall in love.

He asked me to officiate their vows at the top of a Fourteener. I was honored. Despite bringing along a herd of witnesses, the three of us were the only ones to push the last three hours to the summit. Exhausted and gassed from breathing in the smoke from a nearby forest fire, Wayne so very Wayne, in his element, he claimed his joy at fourteen thousand feet.

Fifteen years after that harrowing El Diente attempt, I helped Wayne move from Raton, New Mexico, to Dove Creek, Colorado and found myself driving through Rico, the dispatch location of my search and rescue team. Deep in the San Juan Mountains, Rico has no stop light or sign. I happened to pull behind a fire department vehicle, so I followed it to the station.

I knocked on the door. A young firefighter answered. I explained why I was there—to thank anyone who may have been part of my rescue all those years ago.

She smiled and welcomed me inside. "Let me get our team lead, Ben."

I greeted Ben with a handshake. It only took a moment of recollection to remember that vibrance and strength, even if his age threw me off a bit. Ben was the one I had met coming off the mountain.

"I remember you!" he exclaimed, his expression alight. "You were my first mountain rescue! Ankle, right?"

How unlikely that Ben would still be in Rico, having remained from rookie to team lead. What a gift all those years later to reconnect and express my gratitude. We had a great talk, and he filled in some details that I had been unaware of in my semi-lucid state. Ben had been so anxious to reach me before they called off the search for darkness that he sprinted ahead of his team, something for which he was later disciplined; he simply wanted to optimize the remaining moments before nightfall. In his exuberance, he accidentally startled a man on the trail who raised a large stick he'd been carrying to defend himself. Ben told him, "You'd better think twice. There's a team of people coming up behind me to get a guy off the mountain."

To Ben, I expressed my deepest gratitude for his service and asked if I could take his picture. He gathered everyone in the station to come outside in their turnout gear. His team posed near the banks of snow piled high around the station. It was an emotional moment for me. Such debt is hard to put into words. To Ben, I was the skinny albatross guy, the ankle call, his first rescue. To me, Ben represented life, an extreme expression of love. To put the self in harm's way for strangers is extraordinary. I cannot say for sure if Ben was the one who answered my call on El Diente. Likely, it was a team member. Together, they gave me hope and courage.

And life.

Chapter Eleven

Fifteen years into the quest

In July 2009, Lincoln and Bross Peaks allowed me to visit their summits. Many quest climbers try to scoop up numerous peak accomplishments all at once in this Mosquito Range, as so many Fourteeners are in such close proximity. I planned to save Mount Democrat as my last Fourteener because it was easier and shareable with family and friends. Lincoln and Bross, peaks forty-nine and fifty on my list, were fairly unremarkable.

Mount Lincoln was named after the sixteenth president in 1861, the year he took office. Some think the eastern cliffs resemble the

Lincoln Memorial, built much later in 1914. The story goes that naming this peak triggered those who did not align with the famous Republican's political ideology, and opponents pushed for the naming of nearby Democrat twenty-two years later. Lincoln is a terraced slope with deliberate trails low and an upper exposure where hikers cobble out their experience. At the pyramid-mound summit, there is little danger, nothing more than a class two challenge and a handful of interesting features along the way, including deer and wild horse tracks and signs that warn of potential collapse hazards from old mines.

Bross is a similar ascent, with lignite beds, shard rocks, coarse yellow, gray, and white grit and sandstone. Named after William Bross, a mine owner from nearby Alma just after the Civil War, Bross is generally a dry, bald landscape, short and steep, with crazy-intense wind and some soft summer snow at higher elevations. Much of Bross remains on private land.

As with all the Rocky Mountains, Lincoln and Bross were shaped by what had come before and impacted everything that came after. Change happened gradually, as to almost not even happen at all, but the summation shift proved tectonic.

I liken my Project Children bonds to such a phenomenon. The Irish children who came under our roof, and the ones I placed into Colorado host families, these innocent souls, had already been eroded and swept by their chaotic environments. And though they were with us for weeks, not hundreds of thousands of years, the collective shift in my inner peace was life-altering.

Goodbyes were particularly painful, tearful even, especially early in sponsoring. Our bonds surpassed merely enjoying their company and unique perspectives on their melodious accents. Selfishly, they became family, and we all fell in love with them; though, of course, we knew they had parents and family who loved them in Ireland. Not so selfishly, we knew they enjoyed security in America and believed it to be unfair to ask their young hearts to pack that newfound peace away to return home to violence. As Mark Belford's family experienced, connections endured across many summers, and some families took on tremendous emotional and financial burdens to protect the Irish children and their futures.

The reaffirming process of the program was that these children became adults who stayed in touch with their host families, experienced something positive about America and became mini ambassadors to their nation, and, when faced with the choice to pick up a stone to throw or indoctrination into sects, the overwhelming majority chose peace, time and again.

I will not be like them.

And as for me, *I will not be like him.*

In a strange synchronicity, our Project Children ambassadors packed healing into our hearts, into my old heart, and it was only fair that I honored them, moving forward.

Susan Young came from an Irish-Welsh Catholic upbringing in New Jersey, where a strong work ethic was required to keep food on the table and a roof overhead. At the height of The Troubles, Susan connected with her roots by becoming involved with Project Children. The first child she hosted, Patrick, landed at Washington National Airport so very thin inside his Confirmation clothes. He came from the poorest part of Derry. Quiet but inquisitive, Patrick slowly emerged from his shell. His food preference expanded from French toast with ketchup to more palatable American and Irish dishes, allowing him to gain thirteen pounds over their summer together. In time, Patrick was vulnerable to Susan and opened up about being raised in a single-parent home by an alcoholic mother.

Susan hosted many Irish children during subsequent summers, but Patrick was never far from her mind. Six years on, when she hadn't heard from him, she made a trip to Derry, to his old address, to try to find him. Those who knew Patrick shared the terrible news that he had not reacted well after his grandmother passed and had taken his life.

She grieved him like the loss of a son.

To heal, she remained in more vigilant contact with the children she had hosted. She also sponsored a Derry soccer camp, something Patrick would have loved, and summer camping trips to Virginia Beach, VA, for the Project Children kids while they were hosted in northern Virginia.

I ran across a Project Children application for a young boy with nine siblings, all in protective services, and chose him to come to Colorado. Having the opportunity to place two boys, one Protestant and one Catholic, both from broken homes, with a family of three boys in Longmont, Colorado, presented a wonderful learning experience for all. The letter I received from the host family captured the vision of what I hoped for these children.

The experience far exceeded our expectations. Adam and Martin became good friends, and I gained an entirely new perspective on their conflict at home. They were interested to know so many young people here who had parents who were mixed Catholic and Protestant but even more alarmed at the number who didn't care. They finally seemed to understand that reli-gious affiliation was not critical to deciding with whom one could associate.

I will never forget how Adam and Martin explained to my children what the fully armed Land Rover police vehicles in Northern Ireland looked like—caged in metal around the glass and an automatic weapon on top. When my youngest son said, 'It must be really cool to live there,' both Adam and Martin reacted angrily. Adam, the older boy, explained to my son that home was really awful and not cool at all. Adam told him he was very lucky to live in a place where he was never forced to stay inside his home. Martin quickly agreed and said it would be 'cool' if all the troubles could just end."

In the summer of 1999, I contacted *The Denver Post* to see if they would like to do a story about Project Children and the kids visiting Colorado. They sent a reporter to a gathering at a host family's home.

In the article "Northern Ireland Kids Find Peace," eleven-year-old Kevin Connolly talked about how he'd seen gas bombs and watched police shoot people on his street in Belfast. He described the view from his back garden window as littered with burned-out cars, broken bottles, and stones. "My daddy didn't think I would get along with the Catholics, but look at him." Kevin nodded toward his new-found friend and tossed him a ball. "He's Catholic, and we get along."

For most children who came to America, the departure from long-held prejudices wasn't automatic. When the day arrived to say farewell to the children, our host families gathered at the Denver airport. One host mother pulled me aside to relay her conversation with her Irish charge, Shane, a Catholic boy from Craigavon, Northern Ireland:

"Shane, do you have any Protestant kids you play with back home?"

"Ah no, they're for thumpin'," he declared.

Taken aback, the host mother told Shane that the family on their street, whose children he had played with all summer, were Protestant.

"No way!"

She then chronicled all the children Shane had befriended over the summer who came from Protestant families.

He couldn't believe it. He assumed they were all Catholic kids.

"Well, I like 'em!" Shane declared.

"Remember that when you go home," his host mother said.

One of the most memorable children to visit Colorado arrived my summer of Saint Mary's Glacier. Declan McKerr's expression in his small school photo, stapled to the form, clearly conveyed *Choose me or not. I am who I am.*

Declan came from Lurgan, where Catholics lived on the north end of town, and Protestants lived on the south side. He had dark brown eyes and brown hair. His bio described him as a shy, friendly, and kind eleven-year-old interested in art and basketball. I selected a host family for him with a single mother, Lynne, and three children. Lynne was an art teacher at a local Catholic school.

As always, I called the host family a few weeks into the child's stay to check in. Lynne told me Declan was a quiet young man, not at all talkative, but she and her kids were beginning to connect with him. She had also discovered he had a dislike for many types of food, except dessert. Lynne told me about a comical moment when she was trying to get Declan to eat his vegetables with some insistence. Evidently, the pressure was too much, and he replied in exasperation, "Auch, woman!"

We shared a laugh, and I vowed to make sure we offered dessert when we got the host families and kids together. Thinking this might be a good time to seek media attention for Project Children, I contacted Channel 9 News to see if they would be interested in meeting the children. Their response was to send news anchor Cheryl Preheim and a cameraman to tape an interview with the children at my home. I chose Declan for the interview.

The result wasn't what I hoped.

He wasn't very talkative, giving only one-word answers to her questions, so the segment didn't air, but one question generated a longer, memorable response.

"What did your father say to you when you came to America?" Cheryl asked.

"He said I wouldn't get along with Protestants," said Declan.

"What will you tell him when you go back?"

Declan glared at her as if he were looking at his father and said, "I'll tell him he was wrong!"

His reply was a stunner and caused me to think that we had been successful in reaching another child. Boys like Declan grew into men with strong convictions, men who would be fiercely peaceful. As it turned out, Lynne had just the right patience and understanding to loosen the bands of a tightly wound boy. I was so thankful for the love her family shared with him.

When Declan left, no one knew a seed for music had been planted in his soul. Years later, Declan reconnected with Lynne through an email list from a Burritos to Go fast food shop in Broomfield, Colorado, that had one of her son's names on it. They kept in close touch after he reached out.

During my first trip to Northern Ireland, I also contacted Declan. He invited me to hear him play at a pub in Belfast. I was unprepared for his talent. His command of the guitar was off-the-charts brilliant. His ability to sink into a melody reminded me of Deep Purple's Ritchie Blackmore—intricate, fast, passionate.

Unbeknownst to us all, while Declan was staying with Lynne, listening to her preferred music of Jimi Hendrix and Carlos Santana inspired him deeply. He learned how to play when he returned to Ireland. Fifteen years later, he told me more about his Project Children experience and his journey to musicianship.

When I came back from America, it took some time to realise what Lynne had actually done for me. I wasn't so appreciative at the time, but as the weeks flew by, I only wished to be back. She took me to so many beautiful places. I think I was too young, and I soon realised I was socially awkward.

I was going into junior high that summer. Things changed very quickly. I was now in an 'all boys' school. I thought it would have been hard to get by in there, but I soon made friends with one thing in common: we all loved music. Heavy music. At the time, I was listening to Black Sabbath, Jimi Hendrix, Led Zeppelin, and Pink Floyd. We were the oddballs in school, with our long hair, sewing patches on our school bags and uniforms to look different or cool.

I was always infatuated by the guitar. I grew up watching my uncle play guitar in his Irish Rebel band. I asked for a guitar for Christmas in 2003. I got one, and it was right-handed, like most are. I discovered I was left-handed player. After about five minutes of being upset, my dad said, "Jimi Hendrix was left-handed. Just switch the strings around." So that's what I did. It was a cheap guitar. It sounded awful. After a few weeks of setting it down, I overheard my dá say. "I'm going to get him lessons, and if he gets better, I'll get him a proper left-handed guitar."

This inspired me practice more.

I soon met my guitar tutor, Sam, a Protestant who worked with my father in a carpet factory. Sam had gone to the Guitar Institute in L.A. and had jammed with many great artists. He knew his stuff. He was hard on me the first few lessons, as my hand positioning was awkward. Not so fluent, if you will. He gave me something hard to learn and said, "I'm giving you two weeks at this. If I come back in two weeks and you haven't learned this, then you should take up drums instead."

I learned the piece. Soon, all my friends wanted to play guitar. In fact, every one of my friends picked up an instrument that year. We all practiced like mad. It was either that or go out and throw stones at police—in my estate, anyway. I was later diagnosed with having Asperger's syndrome, which explained me being socially awkward, but it also helped in my obsession to play guitar as good as I wanted. My teachers let me bring the guitar into school so I could practice during recess.

After junior high, I went straight into work, scaffolding, doing anything to get money for more guitars and amps and equipment. I even taught my boss to play guitar. Nowadays, music is my main job. I play four gigs a week, and I am part of an acoustic duo named Gypsy's Wish. I also play guitar for a hip-hop artist named Jun Tzu. I have experienced many things through music and met many great players. It's the only true source of freedom and expression I have. That I will ever have.

Artists are mystics and travelers. They spend their lives seeking to connect to the source of existence, a wavelength or sound, that elusive tone.

I am hesitant to allow others into my beliefs about travelers—not because I fear judgment or the possibility that such things don't exist—but because to know such things risks siphoning away the magic.

The term is not associated with any one person who goes on a geographical journey from point A to point B. Rather, I use *travelers* as a catch-all word to describe the people who move in and out of our lives with a greater significance and a near-mystical quality. These individuals bring a synchronicity of experience, a gift that transcends perspective, a thread of connection to the universe that is easy to overlook. If we see them, they are mentors; if we sense them, we might call them spirit guides, angels, relatives who have moved on, or even pond nymphs who dance among the lilies. We attach to them whatever our belief system allows, but they help us reach a higher consciousness and exist to move us.

Children are open to such travelers. Before the world coaches them on what is real and imagined, their innocence acts as a super-highway to all that is possible. As adults, we spend our lives trying to regain that wonderment, channel the right kinds of energy in the right direction, and open ourselves to the existential answers of life.

When I think about Declan, I think about what might have been the absolute travesty of a musician-to-be pulling the trigger of a gun and taking the path of hatred. It's unthinkable that someone with so much potential, so many natural and learned gifts, might have taken to the streets in violence had he not experienced something different in America.

Choose me or not.

I wanted to choose them all. The longer I was involved in Project Children, the more obsessed I became with doing more. We were making a difference—a *real* difference—but peace did not come fast enough—for them or for me.

Over my years of involvement in Project Children, I placed approximately one hundred fifty Irish children into Colorado host families. Not once did they mention religion in any of their frequent reconnections with me.

In America, they learned that we lived in non-sectarian ways. On any one street in America, they encountered neighbors who were Jewish, Muslim, Catholic, a vast and nuanced spectrum under the umbrella of Protestantism, and maybe even Buddhist or atheist. Relationships were not defined by faith, yet to whatever degree it existed, faith was respected in all relationships. Many Irish children did not know any other belief systems beyond Catholic and Protestant existed. They made mental notes, filed them for later, and then realized the stark contrast when they went home. No longer did they desire to put new acquaintances and friends into sectarian boxes the way their parents and grandparents did. They realized that sectarianism is a learned attitude, and they set about unlearning its toxicity.

Although at Project Children's inception there was an intent to lean into a deliberate framework regarding placing one Catholic and one Protestant child together, the religious climate in America was looser, less strident. Some host families identified as churchgoing, but many did not or had fallen away from the faith of their childhoods. That didn't unqualify them as inspiring host candidates; that simply made them an authentic representation of the climate of religion in America. In truth, the departure from any kind of framework based on bringing the sects together became the very thing that freed the children to think about others in terms of things other than organized religion.

During their time with host families, the children learned to loosen their hold on their identity tied to Catholicism or Protestantism. Understandably, they were cautious about revealing such factions within. However, when they grew comfortable and felt safe, the bandage loosened, and they'd bleed out how strongly they felt about the issue. Their identity and sense of home were so enmeshed in their political-cultural sect that altering their strongly held narrative regarding the enemy felt like a betrayal of the country. For many, it took years after their Project Children experience to process the dissonance of it all.

Certainly, not every Project Children match was ideal. The program encountered its fair share of issues. Any time thousands of people from all cross-sections of humanity come together, even children, there is bound to be adversity: children that went home and gave into the violence, assaults, and even one tragic drowning. Coordinators simply handled these unfortunate, one-off situations with discretion and care.

Once, a female participant ended up in an interview section of *Good Morning America*. Her father was a hunger striker who later died. During the interview, she stated that if America put pressure on Margaret Thatcher, maybe it would be enough to finally address the situation of hunger and the conflict. Her association with Project Children brought the organization into the political arena, a place it neither intended nor desired to be. Project Children quickly issued a statement to diffuse the situation. The organization clarified that they were bringing hundreds of children out of harm's way for a peaceful summer, not trying to shelter their political views.

These rare occurrences certainly added weight and concern to a coordinator's responsibility. Candidate children filled out a questionnaire on their backgrounds, and host families had one or two pages of questions—tell us about your family. Do you attend church? What *words describe your lifestyle?* Details didn't run much deeper. Nearly always, we aligned genders and ages to other children in the household, and tried to assess how a guest child might fit into the family structure. Early on, I had matched a girl to an empty-nest couple in Vail. She was lonely and homesick. Eventually, she bonded with the male over golf—he saw that she had a natural swing, which became their thing. I learned my lesson about the importance of host siblings. Matching children to host families was five percent dossier, twenty percent instinct, and seventy-five percent luck, divine intervention, whatever. I kept in close contact throughout the summers and hoped for the best.

Where intent is pure, results are generally favorable.

As one of fifty coordinators across thirteen states and Washington D.C., I flew to New York to greet the children and accompany them to Colorado. Over the years, Project Children grew to such a massive effort that it required two 747 jumbo jets to bring more than six hundred children to America each summer. Special arrangements were made for arrivals. Coordinators and dignitaries waited in an offsite hangar. We stood with signs naming our state or town so children could easily find the proper coordinator. The air was always electric with anticipation.

Chills always swept over me when I saw the Irish shamrock-painted plane land at Newark International Airport. Cheers and clapping from the crowd fueled the excitement. As the plane taxied slowly to the hanger, two firetrucks, positioned opposite each other, shot arcs of green and orange-colored water over the planes. A New York Police Department bagpipe band played at the stairs pushed to the plane door. Children coming down the stairs, led by Denis, unprepared for such a welcome, had eyes and expressions as touching as anything I had seen. Always, I became so choked with emotion that my composure occupied a narrow precipice. Tears, I allowed.

The kids were so small. The vast majority had never been on a plane, much less to America, a land that both sides of their divide considered a beacon of hope. All the volunteers wanted their visit to be the most memorable and joyful possible. Could we live up to that?

I felt such pride to be part of such an important cause for peace. Every time I witnessed the arrival, it had the same effect on me.

One memorable stormy afternoon arrival, I gathered my large group and let them know that many excited host families waited for them in Colorado. Timid glances and furtive looks said it all. Some carried the fear of uncertainty in their expressions, while others projected an air of confidence and inquisitiveness. A flood of questions came.

"Are there mountains in Colorado?"

"How far away is it?"

"Does Colorado have soccer?"

"How long until we get there?"

"Are there horses/Protestants/NBA players/gold nuggets/Catholics/snowstorms in June/places to get soda bread?" They asked it all. With some, their accents were so thick and unfamiliar, I had to ask them to repeat their questions. Sweet voices on melodic dialects were a Carnegie Hall-caliber concert to my ears.

Host families had been encouraged to write to their host child after matches took place, to introduce themselves and share a little about their lives in Colorado. Many children carried their letters with them. I ensured all had their luggage on the shuttle to the main terminal. I had hoped we'd depart on time, but the storm, stretching from the Gulf of Mexico to Canada, intensified and shut down all westbound air traffic for the evening.

Stranded with the children and no available hotel rooms within miles, I called the company's travel agency and found a hotel with enough rooms to host us. However, it was more than an hour's drive away. The only logical means to get that many children to the hotel was to hire a limousine. At the sight of the black stretch car pulling up to the airport loading zone, the kids' jaws dropped, speechless, before squeals and pogo-stick jumping ensued. They bounded inside, feeling like movie stars.

Arriving at the hotel around midnight, I expected everyone to be ready to go to bed. But many were still wound up. For the next two hours, I roamed the hallways, trying to keep the girls from harassing the boys in their rooms. Finally, at around two in the morning, they went to sleep. The rest didn't last long, as we had to leave for the airport at 5:30. Due to the many cancellations the evening before, I couldn't get us all on a direct flight to Denver. We needed to connect through Chicago. By the time we landed that next afternoon in Denver, we all looked and sounded like Rashers Tierney, the raggedy hero of the Irish show *Strumpet City*, on a bender.

That summer, I learned that major league baseball was not a high-interest sport for the Irish. By the third inning at a Colorado Rockies game, most of the kids were asleep in their seats.

Coordinating pint-sized guests from Northern Ireland was always an adventure, but it was nothing compared to welcoming children into our home. Kelly Ann Toal may have been our first, but subsequent children brought with them unique gifts and lessons and forever changed our family, collectively and individually. Our appreciation for the experience knows no boundaries.

Each of our Project Children girls was like bringing a newfound daughter into our home. Bonds sometimes became strong enough that we would also choose to cover travel expenses for the same child to return the next summer. Natasha, our young lady from the town of Portadown the year before, brought her sister, Jacqueline, with her the subsequent summer. Erin didn't seem to mind having one girl in her bed and another sleeping on an air mattress on the floor for six weeks. I marveled at Erin's welcoming heart.

In general, the Irish girls' expression of tribal identity was either non-existent or more suppressed than the boys. Yes, they were conscious of their religious identity, but boys would readily tell me how they differed from the other side or drop slang for a policeman, a *peeler*, while recounting their history. For some, picking up a stone or bottle and hurling it at a British soldier or policeman was as much of a sport as soccer.

We never judged. Giving them freedom of self-expression was a priority for me. We looked for special gifts and interests and encouraged them in those directions. And we sought out slivers of compassion, peace and joy each day.

The girls loved talking and laughing among themselves. Jacqueline's love for potatoes became legendary in our household. It didn't matter the style in which they were prepared; she wanted them with every meal. One day, Darlene pointed this out, and Jacqueline replied with a passionate voice, "Potatoes are my life!"

Bringing Project Children kids into my daughters' lives brought the greater world past the door. I wanted Erin and Elyse to see themselves as citizens of the world, not just Americans. Preaching peace in Northern Ireland would not have landed the same had the human fallout of war not looked just like them. They would have understood that their father was passionate about peace in Ireland, but it likely would have been more a passing thought than recognizing a plugged-in, bone-deep thirst for change.

So much of my time was spent at airports for my job and at elevation, chasing my quest. Project children hosting allowed me to turn back toward family and partake in deliberate and impromptu experiences that created memories for us all. The newness of the encounters, their accents and behaviors and habits, were endlessly fascinating. As the oldest, Erin had agency and decision power regarding opening our home, and she deliberately marched into new and positive emotional connections for ten summers, from age seven to around sixteen, so her Irish roots and experience are a core part of the woman she became. Her social skills flourished. Our youngest, whose Project Children experience began when she was only three, simply accepted the routine. Her interests eventually strayed to dance, but she always cherished the friendships made each summer.

My daughters also benefitted from the change Project Children brought to me. I never avoided talk of my past, but I also never deliberately poisoned the relationship wellspring between the girls and my family. I liken our Irish guests to pint-sized healers and the trauma of my childhood as an accidental bump on the head, something over which I had no control. Their presence felt like a warm embrace, a calm and reassuring parent energy, saying, "It's okay, Anthony. You're okay." They strengthened me emotionally to be able to speak of my past and eventually confront my parents; if the Irish kids, in the mighty courage of their tiny hearts, could articulate what they had gone through, so too could I.

I became a small part of one of the most successful efforts in human history to break down walls and build bridges. I became a small part of ensuring future generations were not in conflict. I became the best version of myself—the father I wanted as a child, the husband who cherished his wife, the man who championed others and took nothing for granted—because of Project Children.

And I became whole again.

In late March 2001, I made my first trip to Northern Ireland. I wanted to visit some of the towns and schools participating in Project Children. My oldest daughter, Erin, age ten, traveled with me. The plan was for her to stay with my cousin's family in London for the week while I journeyed across the Irish Sea.

One morning at Portadown's Catholic secondary school, Drumcree College, I had the experience of being treated like a dignitary, welcomed into an assembly hall full of students. I was introduced as a coordinator with Project Children and allowed to speak about who I was and answer questions. When it was over, a teacher pulled me aside and asked if I would meet with one of the students on the list to come to America. He had been turned down because he was on Ritalin for his ADHD (Attention Deficit Hyperactive Disorder). The teacher was hoping I might be able to reverse the decision.

Twelve-year-old Kevin Donnelly had a round, smiling, earnest face. We were introduced and settled in folding chairs across from each other. I barely got past saying, "Hello," when Kevin blurted out, in his wonderful Northern Ireland accent, "I just want you to know, I'm not a nut case!"

He wanted to come to America in the worst way.

Further conversation convinced me Kevin was not only quick-witted but also very bright. After our meeting, I called Denis in New York.

"I have a young man here in Portadown who is being turned down because he is on a special medication. Is there anything we can do to allow him to come over?"

Denis said, "Project Children can't take responsibility or the liability for managing a child's medications, but if you find a proper host family who will take responsibility, I'll allow it."

"Worst case scenario, I'll host him. I really like this kid. It will mean the world to him and his family if he can make the trip."

I left Portadown inspired by the vibrancy of the children and their teachers.

I don't remember how I found the Urban family for Kevin. The host mother, Jan, was a school nurse, and her husband, Michael, was a doctor. The three-child family was happy to embrace this friendly, chatty, and inquisitive boy. The summer proved to be a perfect match.

That Portadown afternoon, a short fifteen-minute drive took me to Lurgan to meet Father Kieran McPartlin. I was transported back to my Irish Catholic roots. In a detached building behind the church, the small rectory was almost monastic in its quietness—a great place to write that next sermon. As we sat at the small kitchen table with our tea and biscuits, I said, "Father, it's been a long time since I was in confession. Perhaps my absolution can be getting some kids chosen to come to Colorado and saying a few Hail Marys?"

The priest laughed and said, "Ah, we're much more understanding here in Ireland. I'm sure you've done worthy penance in other ways. Coming to this little corner of Northern Ireland will give you a good introduction to the need to give children a break from the pressures associated with poverty and power. Imagine always having to be on the lookout for danger around a corner, always trying to gauge if the person passing you on the street is a friend or foe. This is a divided community. If I take you to meet a few families, you will see how Project Children is the chance of a lifetime."

Grateful for the tea to lift my jet lag, we headed to the local pub to meet with children and families. As Father McPartlin exited his car, it was like watching the Pied Piper of Hamelin. People flocked to his side. He had earned their love and support. I received an Irish welcome as if they knew me from long ago. Portadown and Lurgan seemed a little less dreary as I said goodbye and headed north.

My final stop was Belfast, where I stayed at the home of the principal of Saint Patrick's Primary School in North Belfast. Riding with her the next morning, I recounted our first experience hosting our first Project Children girl. "Her name was Kelly Anne Toal."

The principal nearly ran off the narrow road. "Kelly Toal? She went to this school!"

My spirits soared. Northern Ireland was small; I didn't think it was *that* small.

"What happened to her?"

"Oh, she's likely in secondary school now. Had a difficult home life, poor girl. No father around to help raise her." She drove into the parking lot. "Well, here we are."

The bunker-like setting of the school took me by surprise. Surrounded by high brick walls and ringed with concertina wire, I wasn't prepared for it to be a building for school children. Cameras recorded over a door entrance that could only be opened by a coded keypad. As we entered, the janitor asked if he could speak with her privately. Returning shortly, she said, "Sorry to say, but we had about a dozen windows smashed out last night. If you wouldn't mind, I will bring you to the office while I tend to that. We'll then go to the library so you can meet our children being selected to come over for this summer." Another secure door led to the administrative offices.

As I waited near her desk, I saw the morning newspaper. On the front page of the Irish News was Kelly Toal.

An uneasy lump formed in my gut, traveled north, and lodged in my chest. I glanced around to ensure I was alone, then lifted the newspaper off the desk.

The picture showed a now-fourteen-year-old Kelly standing amidst the broken glass in her living room alongside her five-year-old sister, Natasha. The article chronicled how Protestant loyalists had come through Kelly's Catholic neighborhood the night before, catching her neighbor outside while on a walk home from an anniversary celebration and nearly beating her to death with axe handles. The same assailants had smashed out the front windows of Kelly's home.

The principal walked into her office.

Dumbfounded, I handed her the paper. "Kelly Toal."

Her jaw dropped; her eyes scanned the article.

How could I be in Belfast on the very day Kelly appeared on the front page of the newspaper, while visiting her former school? The coincidence stunned us both.

"My God. According to this, she lives right up the road? Do you wish to see her?"

I hesitated. More than three years had passed since we hosted Kelly in Colorado. There had been no contact since. I took responsibility for that. There had been so many other children after her and so much responsibility with the program. Still, as our first, memories of her were strong. Why hadn't I done more? I worried about the appropriateness of it all, but I thought of my family—especially Erin—who would want me to reconnect. And, selfishly, I wanted to right the wrong of not staying in contact.

"I would like that."

"Great, I'll have my janitor walk with you. It's only a ten-minute walk."

The neighborhood was exactly as I had read and heard about, regarding hard-pressed parts of divided communities. Two-up-two-down row houses with flags marked it as Irish Nationalist turf. Plywood covered the front window, and steel bars barricaded the outer shell.

I knocked.

Kelly opened the door.

I stepped outside myself. It was her, but not. It had only been three years, but she looked so much older, so wizened, so tired.

"Hello, Kelly. Do you remember me?"

She blinked a few times. Her eyelids widened, her expression shifting from indifference to recognition.

"I…I do." She mapped my facial features and then diverted her attention to the janitor who stood as a bodyguard on the street behind me. "Would you like to come inside?"

We settled in the modest family room. I told her how I came to be in Belfast.

Kelly shifted in her chair and glanced at the door frequently. I did not know if it was my presence or the aftereffect of the vandalism and front-page article. Such publicity likely invited more undesirable attention.

"My mother is upstairs sleeping," Kelly said, "but this is my wee sister, Natasha."

Given her mother's history, she was likely sleeping off alcohol from the previous night. I gave a friendly pint-sized wave to her sister. "I remember her having her first birthday when you were in America."

"She's five now."

I told her about Erin visiting cousins in England. "Next time, I'll come to Belfast with the family, and we can meet again. They would love to see you."

Five minutes. That was all it took to shift the conversation back to discomfort. Kelly had dropped out of school to run the household and look after her little sister. She made little eye contact. I told her I hoped we could remain in touch, but I was careful not to add the pressure of those expectations to her burdens. My heart anchored at her doorway. I left it there and walked back to the school in silence. Not only had I failed her, I wondered what more I could be doing for the children of Ireland.

Upon returning to my London hotel, I called my cousin, Barbara, to see how Erin's stay was going.

"She's been simply miserable since you left."

"What? Why?"

Barbara explained that the previous week, when I had dropped her off, Erin had paid more attention to the adult conversation than talking with her cousins. She had heard me talk about past violence in Northern Ireland, a summation over many years, but something she believed was the current state of danger. By the time my cousin recounted the aftereffects on Erin, I was in a puddle between my shoes.

"She was afraid you'd be killed while traveling up north and that she'd be stranded in England with no one to care for her," Barbara said. "Quite distraught and missing you terribly."

I took the next train back to Eastcote.

At the front door, Erin ran to hug me, tears brimming. I had never felt an embrace so unapologetic, so raw, so desperate with unconditional love. I wanted to tell her we'd go right away, back to the hotel, and do something fun, just the two of us—anything she wanted—but my voice failed me. I couldn't push the words past my collapsed throat.

The ride back to London was quiet. We held each other's hands and watched the countryside zoom past.

"I'm sorry I scared you about my trip," I said. "Let's make tomorrow special. We'll get tickets to the Globe Theater to see a Shakespeare play. *Twelfth Night*. Would you like that?"

"Just you and me?"

"Just you and me."

She nodded enthusiastically and smiled out the window.

Seeing a comedic play in the historic outdoor theater lightened the mood. A memory that belonged only to us.

Children take on so much that is not theirs. Just as Erin had wrestled with her role in our trip to England and Ireland, how I had left her behind, and what she believed was her uncertain future, I had taken responsibility for my father's moods, my mother's bruises, and sibling connections built on self-preservation. Both unable to process logical consequences and nuances in minds that had yet to finish growing, Erin and I asked too much of ourselves.

In times of war.

In times of peace.

All the burdens are not ours to carry.

Perhaps it was these teaching moments that made me come awake for brief periods. When Erin was twelve, the Cirque du Soleil show *Allegria* came to Denver. I fell in love with the story of the ringmaster trying to protect his daughter from the world and a growing attraction to a vagabond kid who has stolen entry into the tent to see his daughter sing the song, "Allegria." As their love develops, there is a poignant moment at the edge of the fence to the circus where the girl is wrestling with whether to stay or run after the young man.

Her father asks, "Do you remember when I used to pick you up and carry you on my shoulders?"

"I cried when you tried to put me down," she replies.

"I can no longer carry you on my shoulders," the father confesses.

We bought the DVD and watched it at home. When it finished playing, I was so moved by the moment I picked up Erin on my shoulders, carried her upstairs, and tucked her into bed for what would be the last time.

Six years later, Erin moved away to college. Darlene and I helped move her into the dorm. I was an emotional wreck. As darkness fell and the drive home loomed large, I looked into Erin's eyes. Tears came on like a flash flood through a valley.

"Do you remember the show *Allegria*?"

She nodded, her eyes swimming.

"I can no longer carry you on my shoulders."

We hugged, unable to utter another word.

Chapter Twelve

As a child, my escape was to wander and explore beyond the beaten paths. Climbing seemed natural. Despite breaking my arms four times as a child, heights didn't intimidate me. When I was four, I climbed the rafters of an English cow barn on an old farmhouse my father had rented, lost my grip, and hit a steel pipe on the fifteen-foot fall. Laying there on the cold, hard concrete, pain surged through my arm. My three-year-old brother ran into the house and told our mother I had fallen.

"Go tell him to come inside," she said.

Obediently, Kevin ran back to the barn and said, "Mom said for you to come inside."

Unable to get me to do anything but cry, he ran back inside and told her I couldn't get up. Out he ran again.

"Mom said for you to get up and come inside."

Back in my brother went.

After the third round, I was finally taken to the hospital and placed in a cast.

The break was so bad, the arm had a u-curve to it. The cast remained on for nearly three months. Once released from its cage, my arm floated on air. With my left hand, I pulled it down. This happened a few more times before it finally remained at my side. I had become so accustomed to holding the cast away from my body it had become an involuntary action.

My three younger brothers might tell the story differently—the two middle ones, certainly, because we drifted apart over matters that largely seeded that late summer of my twentieth year. Time is not an equalizer; it's a felon that steals the fourteen-carat gold memories and leaves the rest like tacky junk inside an old claw machine—loosely tossed together, forgotten at the edge of the carnival grounds, and operated on currency that no one carries anymore. Every now and then, sharp metal teeth pluck an imperfect memory from the pile, only to drop it again because the grip was tenuous.

After his fight with the Army major in Vietnam, who knew karate and knocked Dad out with a chop to the neck, the incident landed him stateside, the body bags flown out of Cu Chi still haunted him. He filled his days with paperwork and a steady paycheck and—likely—a flask sloshing around in the back of his desk drawer. He stretched tall and taffy-thin, spit words with a rural accent, and went out of his way to help others so long as they weren't in the trenches with him behind the fortified tan siding of our house.

That evening—*the* evening—was tucked inside a long and sticky August. Routine at its outset, our family meal unfolded as always: no one speaking, depressing news blaring from the television in the next room, cold pork chops, and heated words—*bastard, bitch, go fuck yourself.*

As we downed our dinner, words cut deeper.

I've had enough of this shit.

You make me sick.

You're not a man. You're a bully.

Forks clanged against plates. Chair legs scraped.

Mom fled to the living room.

Dad followed.

In the summer of 2010, I was training for my yearly Fourteener run when I hit a familiar sharp right curve on my bike with an unfamiliar outcome. I crashed onto the concrete so hard that my foot, shoulder, and head sustained injury. Fortunately, I had an audience to my catastrophic wipeout: a handful of guys out on the fifteenth hole of their weekly golf game. One of them was a paramedic, and they had ice. They loaded me up on their golf cart with all my injuries in a cold pack and drove me to the clubhouse. By the time Darlene arrived to take me to the hospital, my ankle looked like an inflated balloon.

Multiple X-rays confirmed that I had broken bones in my ankle and shoulder. I also had a gash in my head that required staples, and I sustained a concussion. Fourteener plans dashed for the season, I called Wayne to break the news.

"All you had to do was tell me you didn't want to hike with me," he said.

My yearly camping plans with Curtis were also derailed. Wheelchair and crutch-bound, there was no way I would be able to sleep in a tent. He had already booked his flight, so we made the most of it with a hotel camping trip. With my cast propped up on the car's dashboard, we headed west, checked into a wheelchair-accessible room, and spent our days driving to high plateaus and overlooks, where he propped me up in a folding chair that reclined. Curtis would have made a great nurse. Already, he was the best brother I could have asked for.

And as Warren Miller said each time he closed out one of his ski movies, "If you don't do it this year, you'll be another year older when you do." Nevertheless, I intended to achieve my quest and not represent Warren's second most famous quote: "If at first you don't succeed, failure may be your thing."

Dad landed relentless blows on Mom before we could react.

This time, we weren't little boys crying, "Daddy, stop!" We were teenagers and young men. Still, it took all his sons to pull him away from her.

He thundered into the bedroom and slammed the door.

We believed that to be the end—as predictable as potatoes in our Irish diet. The bedroom was his space to cool himself. He was quiet; the worst had subsided. We drifted and settled in the adjoining living room. Someone turned down the television. In the quiet, my eardrums vibrated from the afterburn of shouts. Such incidents were always a bell that could not be unrung. No one spoke.

Moments later, Dad charged from the back room with a single-shot bolt-action German Mauzer rifle. Left hand on the stock, right hand on the trigger, he rammed the muzzle beneath his chin. And he laughed. Like the sideways giggle you make when exiting the Tilt-a-Whirl so your friends don't think you're weak, but there's an entire nauseating trip around the world you're suppressing beneath the skin.

Shouts in the room smothered any words he may have uttered. Likely, some of the cries were mine—*Stop! Don't do this!*—but this memory is a piece of tacky junk: lingering at the fringes, surrounded by sharp metal teeth, somewhere loose between the real and the imagined. Amid the chaos, I only remember absurdity creeping in.

What will the ceiling look like, splattered in his blood?

Will it get on me?

And the notable silence in the room.

Mom said nothing.

Properly recovered from my injuries and a bit more cautious that summer of 2011, Wayne and I tackled Lake Como Road in his replacement truck. This time, we drove halfway up the Lake Como Road and carried fully loaded backpacks the rest of the way. Our 50-pound packs included our tent, sleeping bags, stove, food, water, clothes, and day-packs for a three-night base camp. The hike to the alpine Como Lake at twelve thousand feet, took about three hours.

On the way, we encountered a group of people coming down the road so quickly they were almost trotting. One had a knife in his hand, his eyes wide. They told us a bear had been following them down and had harassed them so badly at their campsite they decided to leave the area. Sure enough, as we looked up the road, there was the bear.

As the hikers scurried on, Wayne and I watched the bear's movements for a few minutes. The bear left the road, so we quickly journeyed ahead. At the lake, we met more campers who told us about problems with the bear. It had come into several campsites during the night and took what food it could find, even reaching food roped into a tree. Those accounts convinced us we needed to hike farther, above the tree line and lake, and camp closer to the base of one of the mountains, avoiding any potential bear issues.

At the basin to the Blue Lakes, over twelve thousand feet in elevation, we set up camp well away from Como Lake, the other campers, and rumors of a rogue bear. The night beside a stream coming off the smaller drainage lakes below the peaks was uneventful and restful. In retrospect, I'm not sure how the site guaranteed our security because a bear can go anywhere it wants, and we had no defense of bear spray or weapon.

Starting early the next morning, we reached Blanca Peak's summit at around ten. After a short break, we hiked over to Ellingwood Point. The scramble between the two peaks involved descending about five hundred feet while looking for solid rock or crease lines in the mountain where we could begin our route up from a lateral line of the ridge. With great weather, we successfully summited both.

With confidence high and plans to tackle yet another Fourteener the next day, we moved our campsite near another stream at the base of Little Bear Peak's west ridge. If we stayed out of the tree area, where many campers were, we would have less likelihood of encountering the bear.

We had just settled into our new camp, water boiling for our freeze-dried meals, when a large brown bear emerged from the woods and ambled toward us. The stream may have been a hopeful barrier for us, but it was no physical barrier for what looked like a grizzly. It splashed through the water, straight toward our campsite. Wayne and I shouted and waved our arms like lunatics. The brown-colored black bear turned back and disappeared into the trees.

At dusk, the bear returned, splashing toward us. Again, we made enough racket for the animal to reconsider. The bear retreated across the stream.

Wayne and I decided it wasn't safe to remain in our tents. We placed what little perishable food we had under rocks several yards away from our tents, gathered our sleeping bags and pads and a plastic tarp, and headed to our previous camping site, using light from our headlamps to gingerly pick our way over the rocky ground. We found a large, flat outcrop of rock next to a stream, laid out our sleeping pads and bags, and placed the tarp over us.

Late that evening, a thunderstorm gathered over the mountain basin and poured rain. Lightning flashed all around us. Pulling the tarp over us more tightly, as it rained for the next two hours, I joked to Wayne, "I can't believe the big bear is keeping us from climbing Little Bear!"

At daybreak, we gathered our sleeping gear and headed back to our tents. There was the bear! We shouted him off again, but he had done his damage: shredded daypacks, ripped holes in our large packs, busted open energy drink that I'd failed to take out, and a split T-shirt—

one of my favorites from an Irish Pub called Fado's. On the back, in Gaelic, it read *Ol Ceol, Ajus, Craic,* which meant *Music, Drink, and Fun.*

Taunting words. The moment was anything but music, drink, and fun.

Gear soaked from the rain the night before, and without daypacks to put hiking gear into, we had no choice but to abandon our effort to summit Little Bear. We headed down the mountain. My available free time to return was gone. The final two peaks of my Fourteener quest would have to wait another year.

The rifle incident did nothing to dissuade Dad from gathering up all his depression, the chemical imbalances in his brain, and his traumas and unleashing them on his family. After another episode of domestic violence, the police wanted to question him.

Just a few questions, they said. It'd be easier down at the station, they said.

Your son can ride with you, they said.

Dad and I exchanged few words in the back of the patrol car. He straightened his unkempt hair a bit. I studied passing landmarks as if I would never travel this same road twice.

At the station we entered and exited through locked doors. I followed without sound, without question, because that was what good Irish boys did. The lead officer stopped in a corridor and pointed past an open door.

A holding cell.

Realization dawned on my father. It didn't matter that they'd said the questions would be easy. It didn't matter that their son had tagged along as a buffer against the threat of some extreme and undesirable occurrence or that he stood witness. His eyes widened the way Mom's often did when he drank too much, stood from his recliner, booze lengthening his threats.

Dad railed against three uniformed officers.

And lost.

In the scuffle, they stripped him of his clothes. It's hard for a man to maintain his dignity in front of his son with his limp body parts battling like salmon against a concrete stream. It's even harder for a son to see his father in a padded cell, deconstructed to his fundamentals of inhumanity: savage breath, barbaric flaws, a violent coldness in his blood.

I stepped back, the distance both welcome and feared. Again, my heart did not know its place and lodged itself in the protective space of my throat.

I don't remember the ride home in the patrol car beyond an internal vow.

I. will. not. become. him.

Dad remained in jail for the weekend. Mom had taken back her control. And there came a divide, an innocence lost. Before jail and after jail.

Never again did he raise a hand to her.

Medical records from that day and a subsequent emergency room visit for a one-car automobile accident revealed a history of depression, substance abuse of Valium and alcohol, and a recommendation for vocational counseling and psychotherapy. *It should be noted that the man is not considered a heavy drinker, but does apparently overreact very much, even to small quantities of alcohol. This could well be the basis of organic brain disease. Patient states he is not a danger to himself.*

I guess they believed him.

He self-reported to his attending doctor that he intensely disliked his job, wrestled with insomnia, was increasingly impatient, and noticed failures in his short-term memory. His future looked bleak.

As an adult, with the distance of time, I say that he lost his way after leaving the military. He found civilian life challenging and medicated with prescription drugs and alcohol to cope, which only exacerbated his manic swings of anger, depression, and, at times, violence. I suspect the genetic component of mental illness in his mother—at most, he inherited the same, and at the least, he grew into an emotionally dysregulated individual. Early on, the cocktail of genetics and trauma from Vietnam may have explained the way he treated those around him, but those were the days when speaking of such challenges landed someone in a mental institution. Later, he had plenty of opportunities in life to self-reflect. He behaved poorly, held fast to his toxic attitude, and paid the price of loneliness.

Though Dad never set foot on a mountain, he was my first phantom guide. He existed to recalibrate good sense and usher, in those of us who occupied his trench, all manner of pain—spiritual, emotional, and bodily. Often, when I scaled peaks dressed in a brightly colored parka and worn boots, with no space left between the lungs and throat, absurdity crept in, and I'd wish for a brush of blinding snow to consume how I felt toward him. If only he would have apologized for any of those years or actions.

Mountaineers like to believe that when our boots hit remote terrain, we develop the superpower to push the junk aside—that oxygen cleanses and nature heals. But we are liars. For a time, perhaps, my Rocky Mountain high was driven by an angry, alcoholic military veteran in the tangle of mental illness, but it didn't end that way.

I didn't strike out after every Colorado Fourteener to die. Unlike my father, I didn't hold the darkness as my companion. I climbed to escape those shadows. For the most part, I did. I climbed because work consumed my waking hours. Mountains set boundaries I could not. And I climbed to rise out of the numbness of a lifetime of being average. I hoarded life's deviations and kept my accomplishments a secret, lest sharing them gave away their magic.

I climbed to live.

Eventually, I climbed for me.

I held tight to granite and earthen strongholds because letting go was more painful. Sometimes, we are unable to do anything but cry. We fight to hold on, and we fight to let go. Change is never easy. Just like an arm that floats, we hold what was broken away from our bodies and become accustomed to the involuntariness of it all.

But there is also healing in closeness. Four points on a rock face. Brotherly love, once estranged. A daughter's hand and *Twelfth Night* on a summer evening. Sharing the top of the world with a friend. A dark pint of lager on a guitar-soaked melody. Inside a tiny rental car with an anxious-to-get-to-the-next-destination tour guide-slash-author. Darkness best shed in another time and place to allow the light.

Wayne and I tackled Mount Hope, a thirteen-thousand-nine-hundred-foot mountain that challenged us like any Fourteener. The hike involved gaining more than four thousand vertical feet in less than four miles, yet we reached the summit just after noon. The sky was clear as we scanned the horizon for hundreds of miles. We thought we could take our leisure in recharging before coming down. Soon, however, small puffs and wisps of clouds collected in the valley floor and swirled as if in a mixing bowl. Thunder emanated from below. We had to get moving.

Clouds rose and formed over the mountain. We hot-footed our descent toward the tree line, two thousand feet below. Having longer legs than Wayne, I paced ahead.

A hissing sound snagged my awareness. I turned to check the tube of my water bladder for leaking air pressure. Wayne paused ten yards behind me, his straight hair fully extended from his head, all Albert Einstein.

Expecting to get *the big zap*, we bolted and didn't stop until we reached cover an hour later. Only then did we dare laugh. And what sweet tears they were.

Little Bear Peak 14,037' | Mount Democrat 14,148'

Chapter Thirteen

Our return hike up Lake Como Road, with the goal of Little Bear, was uneventful. This time, no bear distracted us. Wayne and I heard reports from a few hikers that forest rangers had to euthanize the bear we encountered the previous year, as he had become too comfortable around people.

Monsoon season had set in. We carefully sorted our equipment. If much rain fell on the peak, the climb through the *Hour Glass* would be dangerous—perhaps fatal. Objective hazards on this stretch of Little Bear are numerous: slabby and steep sections of water-polished rock, a challenging class-four technical climb followed by a stretch of navigating ledges with far too much loose talus. This notorious section of Little Bear has an additional nickname—Bowling Alley. One rock loosened down the wax-like cliff, and you'd take other climbers out like pins.

The route required an initial ascent through a steep couloir for about eight hundred vertical feet before reaching the ridge's crest. Ninety minutes later came Hour Glass. As we feared, water streamed down this mountain section. Settling on the right route was critical. Two descending climbers recommended using the rope anchored at the top of the gully. This rope is often a source of debate—rely on yourself and your experience or a twist of nylon left to the elements and overused, that sometimes comes off in chunks?

As we readied ourselves for the final push to the summit, clouds gathered overhead. Carefully, Wayne and I began to climb the steep and narrow route. As the walls of the gully closed in, we moved higher. I free-climbed briefly on one side wall—a few dozen feet—but saw no easier option.

We crossed over the forceful stream, climbed higher, and searched for the rope. Nothing. Again, we crossed, this time finding the rope soaked inside the waterpour. Clouds gathered overhead. All potential footing was hard and glassy. Rarely had I felt so exposed.

"If it starts raining," I told Wayne, "the rock will be so wet, we'll slide right off the mountain."

Wayne agreed.

Reluctantly, we aborted the effort and headed back down. At the crest's ridge, I noticed the clouds had lifted. There would be no storm, but I still felt comfortable with our decision. Little Bear is considered Colorado's most dangerous standard-route Fourteener. It toys with even the most confident mountaineer's brain and confidence. At the trailhead, we agreed to meet in a few weeks and try again.

Our August Little Bear attempt proved to be the charm. No water streamed down the gully, and the Hour Glass was dry. We used the anchored rope for support and reached the summit quickly. Looking out at the Great Sand Dunes and the other two previously summitted peaks of Blanca and Ellingwood, the view was spectacular. I was one happy dude. Wayne took a picture of me wearing my only headband, inscribed with the words *E Cannabis Unum*. I had picked it up some years earlier at an Army surplus store in Walsenburg, Colorado, and wore it to keep sweat from running down my face. It makes Wayne laugh because it's as close as I get to inhaling anything but fresh air.

The sense of accomplishment I felt on the descent was profound. Four tries on this mountain and so many other Fourteeners that required multiple attempts. We had surpassed the bear, the weather, and Wayne's truck loss, not to mention other obstacles in our personal lives that year.

I had one final peak in my quest, and I planned to make it a party.

Mountaineers are a superstitious bunch. I was no exception.

My baby blue station wagon with faux wood grain panels had been more than my wingman in my quest. The car gave me safety and shelter on cold mountain nights, reliably beat it down the road for hundreds of thousands of alpine miles, and gave me a way to effectively embarrass my daughters in the proper vein of a father. As a high school freshman, Erin was so embarrassed to be picked up in the wagon that she'd dart into the backseat and lay down to avoid being seen. I made sure to drive extra slow for her classmates to properly appreciate the luxury, wood-grained beaut. At three hundred thousand on the odometer, I sold it for fifteen hundred dollars. For a few years, I'd spot it driven around the neighborhood and pine to be back in its driver's seat. Once President Obama's Cash for Clunkers program launched, I never saw the wagon again.

And then, there were the boots.

I should have named them. Spoke to them when I hiked. Buried them. Then again, giving them a persona beyond size twelve, Rocky brand might have been one crazy brain cell too far in my determination to finish my fifty-fifth peak in the same pair I started.

They were Gore-Tex moccasins with traction, the most comfortable boots I had ever worn. Darlene gave them to me when I grew serious about hiking. They gripped wet rocks without slipping and shielded my bony ankles from injury.

Over my eighteen-year relationship with these boots, we disappointed each other. At times, I made false summits or didn't take them all the way due to weather or conditioning. Climbing is nothing if not unpredictable. Sometimes, we both needed to be fixed. Resoling them three times no longer made them waterproof. Because I frontloaded my goals list with easy peaks, more challenging peaks came when the boots had grown tired. But we kept each other. They became a point of conversation when my introversion failed me. They projected loyalty. They were flawed, and so was I. We both understood what it meant to fall short but step forward anyway.

Around peak thirty-five, I wrote the mental script for how peak number fifty-five would go down. I would scale my last mountain in these no-longer-moccasins-with-traction boots, slip them off at the peak, toast them with a bottle of champagne, and pull new boots from my pack for the descent.

At the top of Democrat, that's precisely what I did.

When my first photography-based book, *The 18-Year Quest*, was published, I sent a copy to Mike Brooks, chairman of Rocky Brand boots. He called to thank me and sent me a new complimentary pair of Rocky Boots for my next eighteen-year adventure. His follow-up letter read *I may be a little partial, but knowing our boots were with you on your journey makes your story that much more special.*

After a stressful parental visit to my home, I wrote my father a letter. Writing has always been my preferred method of communication. A letter guaranteed my words would be put out into the universe, that I would be heard—*finally* heard—inside our eggshell relationship. What happened afterward was, perhaps, of little consequence.

I told him that I was happy to allow our daughters to stay with their grandparents, to form bonds independent of me, but that to I would no longer sleep in the home of my childhood. Rather, I would stay in a nearby hotel. From the mountains, I had learned about boundaries.

By this time, his body was racked with smoking-related COPD, heart issues, and arthritis. His body was hunched over, having lost nearly a foot in height. All children go through such things—seeing their parents regress to a helpless state. For me, his weakened state brought a measure of relief. He could no longer hurt me or those I loved. As with Curtis, he never offered me an apology. He never acknowledged the letter. Our invisible barriers—mine of guardedness, his of callousness—remained until his death.

The family elected me to speak at his funeral. I scratched my thoughts on the corner of a paper ripped from the hotel room pad. I felt disconnected. Nothingness.

Almost nothingness.

When his honor guard played taps, the stinging nettles of some distant emotion—maybe longing for what never was, maybe disappointment, never guilt or grief—gathered inside me. As the son of a veteran, it was a beautiful thing to witness.

Forgiveness happens in spaces where opportunity for progress exists. My father tried to atone for his behavior by investing in college funds for his grandchildren's future. My girls appreciated this support and loved him as their grandpa. I am grateful to him for trying to love them in the way he knew best. Because my father is gone, there will never be forward movement for me. Circling back is something I'm no longer motivated to do.

People go, but the things they did never really leave. Such complexities exist in the human heart. Mostly, I want my daughters to know that there was once a little boy who tried his best to navigate his early darkness by chasing the light at the top of the world. They may even write me a letter someday.

I will do everything I can to celebrate such an extraordinary bid at connection.

At sixteen, I visited Ireland for the first time. I saw shades of green I didn't know existed. Brightly painted doors in the *bailes* outside Dublin welcomed us. We met only friends, even if they were strangers. My first alcohol was an Irish coffee in a moody pub.

Tom introduced me to the sacredness of such a place, where winter storms blew for days on end, and the people known as *the keepers* protected the land and its stories. Once, after discovering and photographing a massive oak tree growing out of a ring fort in a wooded grove, a farmer came upon him and exclaimed, "Auch, Jesus! Tell me, please, ye didn't mess with that tree." When Tom tried to explain, the man's continued tirade cut him off. "God, man, I don't want ma cattle go'n lame, all because ye took photographs of that place." It was only when Tom told him that he had placed three silver coins under one of the roots to appease any trouble he may have caused that the man calmed down.

"Thank God there's one good yank runnin' round Ireland who knows somethin' of the old ways."

The farmer was also a Trinity college-educated man with a master's degree, thus proving the Irish veil between logic and belief was a bit opaque. A possible curse had been avoided was all there was to know about that circumstance.

Tom was one of them—Irish Celts who centered the earth and dialed into its frequency.

On our journey through Ireland, he introduced me to storytellers like Eddie Lenihan.

Eddie was an Irish man who cared deeply about the land and its sacred realms. When the Irish road commission planned to cut down a fifteen-foot whitethorn bush, locally known as the Fairy Bush of Latoon, to build a bypass road from Limerick to Ennis, Eddie knew action had to be taken. Locals believed the site to be a gathering point for fairies from Munster on their way north to fight the fairies in Connaught. He raised such vehement opposition that the road was split in two to preserve the bush. At his home, I was amazed to see shelves with audio cassette tapes of decades of such stories shared by local village people throughout Ireland. Tragically, by the musty smell, I surmised they were decaying. Eddie had offered them to the Irish Historical Society to translate and preserve, but they expressed no interest. To me, it was like discarding the DNA of a culture, time capsules of Irish identity as rich as any people.

Before we left, we visited a three-ring fort and a pair of trees Eddie called, *The Boys*. These were friends he talked with as naturally as any boys at a bar, but they were inside the ring of the fort and deserved respect.

Nearing the end of our two-week journey, our last night was at an inn next to the Neolithic site of Dowth. The owner shared enchanting stories that added to our journey of two worlds. I knew it would be difficult to leave Ireland, to return to the world of struggle and madness. I had met people who understood how to live life so differently. As we stood in front of Glebe House at dusk, overlooking a beautiful garden and a row of tall trees with Elizabeth, the owner, she shared her nightly wonderment of seeing lights floating along, at eye level, as if guiding the "little people" along their way. She also spoke of nights hearing instruments played as they marched.

After everyone had turned into their rooms that midnight, I was awakened by a drumming sound. I looked out from my second-floor room into pitch blackness. The cadence was like a stick on the side of a drum, but it was rhythmic. I wondered, could it be a bird or another animal hitting a gutter on the roof? The synchronous beat continued for about thirty seconds and stopped. I chose to think it was the fairy folk who had given me a special goodbye.

It took years for me to process everything I experienced on that journey through Ireland. A new me was unearthed; it took the gift of a traveler and a storyteller to unveil it. I'm forever indebted to Tom for sharing the depth of his knowledge. Storytelling is a dying art, unrecognized as a proper feature of today's life. In a grandiose minute way, it lends sacredness to the trials of life and opens us to its possibilities. Not every spot on the globe is such a place and such gatekeepers, but if you've been to a landscape where there is little footprint of man and you never wanted to leave, you've probably had such thoughts too.

Ireland still calls me back. I want to hike one or all the thirty-two high points in the country and let my new boots soak into the soil. I want to teach others that if they have a heart and a willingness to respect nature and who and what came before them, they will be invited into realms where nature turns mystic. And, at the true end of my journey, I want my ashes spread on the famine road near the stone wall. That is, if my family can find it. I've been back to search several times; it's like it never existed.

In so many ways, I am still that wandering boy of five at the pond outside Yateley Hall. He is a bit frozen in time. He desires a life of adventure and peace. I'd wish him a good journey and not much else— certainly nothing that would make his life easier or less bumpy. For it is in the lilies and the dark pools, the beginnings and endings, the firsts and lasts, and all the glorious tragedies in between that we connect to the magic of who we were meant to become.

Two weeks after summitting Little Bear, I reached the final peak— the last of my Fourteeners. Mount Democrat is a class two climb that begins at the tree line surrounding Kite Lake. The hike begins with a long, slow ascent to the mountain base, then gathers up a switch-back, narrowing trails, a bit of loose rock, and a false summit. For most fitness levels, doable; for two of the people I most wanted to share the day with—Curtis, whose lung capacity had further deteriorated since Wetterhorn, and Elyse, who had sustained an ankle injury in dance—impossible. Their absence left a hole in an otherwise euphoric celebration.

Nine other friends and family joined me: Darlene and Erin, along with a friend of Erin's; Craig, my first hiking companion, and his family; photographer and friend Garrett Mynatt, who captured the end of a long quest with such joy and reverence; and friend Fred Burkelhammer, who encouraged me to join my love of mountaineering to my love for writing. Wayne could not make it that day, but Erin and her friend did a dual yoga pose while holding the sign that read *Mount Democrat*, captured in a fun photograph, that paid proper homage to his significant role in my achievement.

We reached the top in a little over two hours. From my pack, I pulled out my new boots and a bottle of champagne. Others on their own Fourteener quest at the summit joined our celebration.

Democrat split me in two. Relief coursed through me, but the lead pack of sadness for those who had died on their quests—Vince and Daniel—weighed my shoulders. Had I, too, not made it back from a mountain, dying with my boots on, doing what I love, is how I would have wanted to be remembered. Risks I took should have been my end. I am alive, in no small part, due to dumb luck and things beyond our human understanding.

In the quest's early years, especially, disconnection from the world was easier. I couldn't FaceTime anyone from the summit. Push notification sounds did not yank me out of my stream of consciousness. External media left no trace on my internal landscape. Email was in the office, not in my pocket. Cell tower signals for phone calls were sketchy, at best. For those hours, sometimes days, I was off-radar and healing. The arduous pursuit relaxed, rebalanced, regerminated. I did not feel the urge to chronicle my quest beyond a list because it was always about release. I shed; I did not retain more than just an incidental memory here and there.

Uneventful, for any Fourteener, is a charmed day.

Regretfully, I no longer think such disconnection is possible. Even if we have the discipline to take ourselves off the collective radar, our brains and our interpersonal relationships are conditioned to a level and intensity of connectivity that isn't always healthy.

I may still have a few climbs left in this aging body, but most of my ascents are behind me. Fourteeners are a young climber's quest. All the surgeries, all the broken bones, and my body still crossed the finish line. I was a fool in the beginning—scrawling peak names in a journal like a Viking on a conquest. Close call moments, losing climbing buddies, and the body's tolerance for pain shifted my perspective. I now appreciate the smallest beauty on the ascent; it's why we stop to gather our breath. I now glimpse around, not just the paces directly ahead; for the *little people* that bring magic dwell at the fringes. And I now thank nature's spaces that allow me to pass; it's in the mindset of gratitude that nature begins to heal us.

Epilogue

In late August 2016, I discovered profound stillness.

From my campsite the previous night, I hiked my descent. With no trail carved out of the open hillside by previous travelers and only a general sense of destination, the summer colors were a surreal pallet in all directions—columbines, bluebells, and lousewort. Blue lupine, pink fireweed, and yellow yarrow skimmed my knees. For hours, I sat at the edge of Grizzly Creek Canyon on a limestone cliff with a sheer drop-off hundreds of feet to the valley below. The day imprinted my aloneness.

And the earth hummed.

I dismissed it at first. Vast silence is a playground for the mind.

After being a climber for decades, I was well-attuned to blood flow through my arteries. This was different. The ancient primordial hum of the planet moved beneath my skin and along the landscape of my tired muscles.

Every day, all day, ocean waves and earthquakes and pulsing storms ring the Earth like a low-frequency bell. A small percentage of people who hear and feel the planet's vibration chase data to prove the hum exists. To prove they're not the sleep-deprived crazy ones.

One of the most gifted and visionary climbers in history, Jeff Lowe, chronicled the same auditory phenomenon while hunkered down in a snow cave on Eiger, with spindrift avalanches threatening to bury him.

Your first thought: *I'm hallucinating.*

Your second thought: This is me . . . *really* me.

Your remaining thoughts circle concepts like infinity, the world's grandeur pressing your body from all sides, and the universe's expansion alongside your inhales. The humming is a gift that ushers purpose and clarity.

It was a gift I could not have accepted a day sooner. I needed car bombs detonating the residential streets of Omagh in Northern Ireland, an aging body, and a militant father from rural Pennsylvania who never stepped away from humanity's darkest *isms*. And I needed a fellow traveler who shared her story of Welsh mysticism to expand and contract my consciousness like a balloon. Her instructions: *consent to live until you have done what you were formed to do.*

Combined with near-death reminders on mundane peaks, it all made perfect sense.

Jeff Lowe called his experience *metanoia.*

I call mine an even trade: *mountains for peace.*

Seven children who participated in the early days of Project Children were killed in The Troubles. The remainder of the more than twenty-three thousand children who came stateside in the program's forty years returned home and planted seeds of hope for peace in Ireland. Between 1975 and 2007, one in every seventy-five Irish citizens had visited America through Project Children.

Stateside, the program swelled to eleven states and the District of Columbia, the latter of which touched high-profile lawmakers and politicians, including Kitty Higgins, Assistant to the President, Secretary to the Cabinet, and later, Deputy Secretary of Labor, who pulled Denis aside at a White House ceremony to honor policemen and encouraged him to tell then-President Bill Clinton of his peace effort in Northern Ireland. The timing could not have been more fortuitous: President Clinton had just become personally involved in negotiating a ceasefire and assigned Senator George Mitchell to the peace process. Years of difficult and painful negotiations had paid off, and the signing of the Good Friday Peace Accord was at hand. Kitty arranged the delegation that flew over on Air Force One to conclude negotiations. The president was so taken with Denis' efforts, he was asked to be part of the delegation.

Denis was twice nominated for a Nobel Peace Prize, was honored by the Pope, made an Officer of the British Empire, and named, along with fellow founder and brother Pat, as *People of the Year* in 1989 by The Rehab Group of Ireland. In 2016, Project Children became the subject of a ninety-minute documentary film, *How to Defuse a Bomb: The Project Children Story*, narrated by Liam Neeson.

Project Children existed and was successful in a social, generational, and political silo. The advent of the internet and smartphones brought worldly perspectives not bound by the constraints of sectarianism to Irish youth. Today, such an experiment, proven successful by Project Children's legacy on the peace process—say, between Israeli and Palestinian children—would likely not have the same impact because the world is too connected. Unfiltered noise is the enemy of peace and healing.

The program's final act is one of opportunity. Project Children continues in a modified form and is aimed at college-aged students and young adults who come to America as interns, stay with host families, and perform community service. Ireland needs future leaders with a broader understanding of how to get along with opposing sides. Participants are ambassadors of Ireland who work in fields ranging from political staff in Washington to engineering and research.

As an afternote, it's important to recognize that peace in a region does not bring immediate peace. In the years after the Good Friday Agreement, suicides for the so-called *Ceasefire Baby* generation nearly doubled. PTSD rates for subsequent children who never even saw conflict remain among the highest in the world. Whereas most nations where wars end involve a collapse in regime and infrastructure, making it impossible to accurately study the aftermath of war on a collective people, Northern Ireland's Troubles were internal and left the nation largely intact. This unique dataset proves peace does not always eradicate a country's problems. Parallels to the way Holocaust trauma was passed down through generations are being examined in academia.

Perhaps that is part of why the Children of Lir statue was placed in the Garden of Remembrance in Dublin, Ireland. Like the children caught up in the power struggles of rulers of the Tuatha De' Danann, Ireland had been held captive for hundreds of years under British rule. At last, the nation was free.

There will always be a human drive to move forward. Reflection pulls us back, but it is necessary for closure. Only when we can ensure the same mistakes won't repeat can we fully surrender to new beginnings.

The wilderness helped me contemplate how to make my life happier and more meaningful.

I have experienced the unexplainable: places that enchant like no other, time that collapses, chance encounters that defy rational cause and effect, and heights that are nothing less than mystical. Over the years, I chased down words to properly define and compartmentalize truths that made sense for my path. I struggled to put it all together until a friend left behind a book at my house.

British television producer Lyn Webster Wilde wrote *Becoming the Enchanter* as a guidebook through the frayed edges of consciousness, Welsh Celtic mythology, and the human cost of misplaced obsessions. Permissive in the way it invited me to centeredness and visions that originated deep inside, the read was a powerful mental stretch I could only absorb for a few pages in one sitting. I lacked the awareness and maturity to accept such a gift in my youth, so I was grateful for its delayed timing. After reading the book's final sentence, I immediately planned a mountain trip to digest its messages.

In late August, I camped at a remote place in western Colorado, which has amazing energy—a canyon so beautiful it makes you not want to leave its edge. My first evening, at a place I had never been to, was up a steep dirt path overlooking Grizzly Creek Canyon that challenged my car to climb. Had it been wet, I wouldn't have made it.

Setting up camp in a stand of trees high above the canyon, I was stunned at the silence and experienced a quietness so loud my ears were ringing from the solitude. There was no wind, no sound—not even an insect's buzz or a bird's chirp. In all my mountain experiences, I had never experienced this level of profound stillness. I felt like Arianrhod, the Celtic goddess of fate, guided me. Wilde describes this stillness as a "sonic boom of quietness." My thoughts wandered to a possible encounter I might have with a bear after seeing signs of freshly clawed fallen logs nearby and bear prints in the soft earth where it had been looking for grubs.

The sense of isolation grew stronger.

As the evening light faded, I heard chatter behind me and turned toward the sound. I saw three owls circling a nearby tree, stalking a squirrel. The chatter continued for some time until it became completely dark, and the owls disappeared. Deep silence returned and caused me to look into the night sky, embracing the sense of feeling small within the universe of space and consciousness. Acute isolation pressed me from all sides.

Daylight faded to darkness.

Could I escape?

Did I need to?

I set a fire for reassurance and warmth, climbed into my tent, and wrestled with the risk of the bear's return. Should I remain there? Open to the spell of Arianrhod or retreat to the safety of my car?

Inside the tent, I placed a pocket knife and hatchet beside me.

That night, I had a profound dream. On a high mountain ridge, in the hallway of an abandoned monastery, I found an old acquaintance, Tom, trying to light a fire—a traveler and guide who once mystically carried me across Ireland. He had imparted so much wisdom about the natives' mysticism that the excess had spilled over into forgotten nothingness. I lamented the loss of our connection. The fire seemed to be a signal to thread together our journeys again.

Later, a thunderstorm stirred me awake. The tent was dark. No creatures stirred. Listening to rain patter against my nylon shell, I pondered the dream's meaning. How had I been so favored by the universe for such a transcendent experience? Before I drifted back to sleep, I brushed my fingertips against the hatchet's handle.

A year later, I traveled to London and met Lyn. She had made the long trip from Wales on my request, and we spent a day walking the city streets, getting to know each other and determining if we shared a common frequency for the mystical. Convinced we did, I gave her a stone from one of my Fourteener summits and asked if she would find a place for it in Wales. I had collected very few of these stones— only certain ones that stood out among the many on a peak. Upon her return home, she wrote me.

Your stone has found its Welsh home!

Yesterday was a beautiful sunny day, but each of our little Arianrhod group had obstacles to encounter before coming: my car was playing up (or was it just the fairies?); Wayland had to say goodbye to his little daughter, moving to Germany with her mother; Sabrina had a job interview; Iris has just moved house. But we made our rendezvous a little late at the place known as Craig y Nos (Rock of the Night) and set off up a steep path through a farmyard full of horses. Iris's lurcher pup, Blossom, was with us too.

Halfway up, we saw a fox, a big, deep red old boy, who turned and studied us before sloping off. Shedding clothes, we staggered up in the unex-

pected heat, not sure whether the stones we were out to find would be easy or difficult to discover. A lark helped us take the right route, and there they were – the seven stones called Saith Maen, some lying down and some still standing up. Next to them was a round crater in the earth, spiraling down like a giant cauldron. Sabrina's guidebook told us that these strange pits are caused by rain and erosion of the earth, but local folklore has it that they are entrances to the underworld and maybe a network of tunnels leading to a massive cave system nearby called Dan yr Ogof. There's a story about a man who was taken away by the fairies who live there, and kept for seven years, emerging with a load of treasure. Maybe Arthur and his Knights are sleeping there, too, but many places in the UK claim that honor.

We dreamed for a while and sensed a guardian and Edge, a lot of power. Were we permitted? We stood around the cauldron, which has a spectacular view of hills and valleys on all sides, and made our sense of scale jump out a few notches. Then we performed a sequence of movements from the Arianrhod work (tell you more sometime), ending by 'making' a cup, signifying 'to give and receive.' We sensed the elemental beings from below responding to us, enhancing our power and welcoming us. I cast your stone into the cauldron, and they took it. We chanted and sang for a while, and it seemed they sang back. We called for them to help us call you to come to Wales! A strange acoustic. The ewes and lambs were intrigued and came to watch.

Wayland, a bit of a mountain goat like you, scrambled down and felt the big stones at the bottom. He could sense something hollow below and maybe water. He had to spiral round the bowl-shaped pit to get back up!

We all felt buoyant and energised by our encounter with this place and its beings.

Cofion cynnes, Lyn

I awoke, the hatchet and knife beside me.

Mist accompanied the dawn, and morning commanded the wild-flowers to stand tall. The profound silence that initially greeted me became a cacophony of nature: the chatter of squirrels, the swish of an owl's wings, the twisting of columbines, bluebells, and lousewort on a breeze.

What followed were the moments that imprinted my aloneness. The day the earth hummed. The vibration was a gift of love from the universe—a reaffirmation of connectedness.

The tethered string of charity and beliefs between stations.

My spiritual sweet spot.

I'm content in a space where I no longer ask questions. Such things defy explanation, anyway. They are to be enjoyed and embraced but not explained.

THE END

Acknowledgments

Wayne McClelland, my hiking buddy for half of my Fourteener summits, was always willing to hike a mountain to help me with my quest. Being his best man on top of a 14er was an honor.

Tom Quinn Kumpf, writer, photographer, and journalist. Never have I met a more diversely talented artist. When I first met Tom, he was documenting moving stories of how PTSD was taking root in the children of Northern Ireland and how they still had an amazing childlike resiliency. Whether he was producing internationally recognized photographs, writing Haiku, or taking me on a mystical tour of his book, *Ireland, Standing Stones to Stormont*, Tom taught me how a master storyteller weaves a tale.

Sometimes we are given the opportunity to meet those who are "travelers"—ones who have accumulated wisdom beyond a lifetime. Lyn Webster Wilde was one such person. Author, BBC producer, and Welsh mystic, Lyn welcomed me as someone who only needed a little nudge to see through the veil. The riddle of the hunting owl makes so much sense now. You will be so missed.

Denis Mulcahy, Chairman of Project Children and retired bomb squad detective with the NYPD, accepted my phone call in 1998 and welcomed me as his Colorado coordinator. Twice, he was nominated for the Nobel Peace Prize. Doing the work of peace and reconciliation under his guidance has brought as much healing to me as it did to the children we hosted.

James M. Lyons, Honorary Consul General for Ireland, was always willing to extend the Irish welcome to my Project Children interns and learn about their summer work experiences. In 1997, Mr. Lyons succeeded Sen. George Mitchell as Special Advisor to the President of the United States and Secretary of State for Economic Initiatives in Northern Ireland and the border countries of the Republic of Ireland. He served in this position until 2001. He was responsible for numerous economic initiatives in support of the peace process. He also served as the United States Observer to the International Fund for Ireland ("IFI"), a diplomatic post to which he was appointed by President Clinton in 1993.

My editor, Laura Mitchell, took what many saw as two stories and found the thread to tie them together. I am grateful for her skill in extracting the emotional memories I kept so close. I am also grateful for her knowledge of how to connect the right designer for the cover and so many other key steps for publishing.

Beta readers Nancy Eaman, Kathy Flood, Linda Koch, Nancy Callahan, and Marilyn Heineman provided invaluable critiques on how to improve the book.

My wife, Darlene, gave me confidence to explore more than the mountains I love, she also helped this London lad, born to an Irish mother and American father, find ways to connect my identity better than the Mother Superior, who, when I was five years old, wrote that I must "be approached with understanding."

My daughters, Erin and Elyse, you inspire me. A scientist and a nurse. You took the best of what your parents offered and built a solid foundation for the future.

Enjoy this book?

You can make a big difference.
Word of mouth is critical to a book's success. Honest reviews bring the attention of new readers. If you enjoyed *Mountains for Peace*, please visit your preferred online retailer and leave a review.
Thank you,
Anthony

About the Author

Anthony Massey is an accomplished author and mountaineer whose love for storytelling and the great outdoors has led him to achieve extraordinary feats. A lifelong adventurer, Anthony is one of an elite club of explorers who have successfully summited all of Colorado's Fourteeners—the state's fifty-five 14,000-foot peaks. His journeys into the rugged wilderness continue to inspire his writing and life philosophy.

In addition to his mountaineering achievements, Anthony is deeply committed to fostering peace and understanding. His experience as a Colorado coordinator for Project Children, working with youth who sought healing and refuge from The Troubles, has profoundly shaped his outlook on life and humanity.

When not scaling peaks, Anthony enjoys spending time with his wife and two daughters and nurturing the friendships formed with the now-grown children who once journeyed from Northern Ireland to Colorado. Through his writing, Anthony invites readers to push beyond their limits and discover the answers to life's most profound questions.

Photos

Author at about one year and parents, Sylvia and Warren Massey.

The Wagon, faux SUV.

A Famine Road to Nowhere.

Best of friends visiting in Portadown, Erin Massey, Jacqueline Loughran, Elyse Massey, Natasha Loughran.

Former Governor of Colorado, Bill Owens, welcoming our Project Children in 1999. Photo credit to Tom Quinn Kumpf.

Statue of the Children of Lir at Garden of Remembrance in Dublin, Ireland.

Author, Anthony Massey.

Original boots used on all 55 summits and various earlier attempts.

DIRECTORY

PEAKS CLIMBED 707-2553

Name	Address	Phone
1 PRINCETON 7/ /94		7-22-95
SUNSHINE/REDCLOUD		7-23-95
3 SHERMAN		7-6-97
MISSOURI		7-13-97
QUANDRY		8-9-97
BELFORD/OXFORD		8-23-97
7 BIERSTADT/EVANS		9-17-97
LONGS		7-4-98
GRAYS/TORREYS		7-25-98
SNOWMASS		8-15-98
ELBERT		8-22-98
NORTH MAROON		8-30-98
11 MASSIVE		9-7-98
PIKES		9-19-98
LA PLATTA		9-26-98
HARVARD/COLUMBIA		10-24-98
YALE		7-2-99
LINDSEY		7-2-00
ANTERO		8-20-00
TABEGUACHE/SHAVANO		8-27-00
HOLY CROSS		9-10-00
HURON		9-17-00
PYRAMID		7-8-01
CASTLE - CONUNDRUM		8-19-01
SOUTH MAROON		9-2-01
4 HANDIES		9-9-01
CAPITOL		9-2-02
UNCOMPAGRE		8-1-03
WILSON PEAK (GLADSTONE)		8-20-03
WETTERHORN		9-3-03
4 HUMBOLDT		9-4-03
CRESTONE PEAK (EAST CRESTONE)		7-2-04
SNEFFELS		8-14-04
CRESTONE NEEDLE		8-15-04
4 KIT CARSON (COLUMBIA 13,980)		9-3-04
MT. WILSON		7-5-05
SAN LUIS		6-13-06
CULEBRA		8-25-07
EL DIENTE		7-11-09
LINCOLN/BROSS		9-2-11
BLANCA/ELLINGWOOD		
LITTLE BEAR		8-12-12
DEMOCRAT		9-2-12
SUNLIGHT		9-5-08
WINDOM/EOLUS		9-6-08
BROSS/LINCOLN		6-28-09

Dates of Fourteener summits.